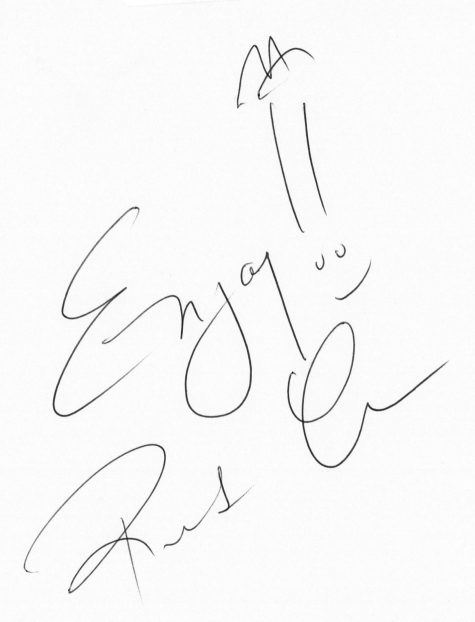

THERE IS STILL Romance in FOOD

Richard Carr, C.E.C.

THERE IS STILL Romance in FOOD

1st Printing, June 2003

ISBN: 0-9740581-0-6

Food Photography by
Len Rothman Photography
Norfolk, Virginia

Additional photography provided by the *Colonial Williamsburg Foundation*. A special thank you to *Mr. Charles Driscoll, Ms. Grofils,* and *Mr. Joseph Roundtree* for their great help to further the cooperation for the advancement of appreciation for the city of *Williamsburg* and the *Colonial Williamsburg Foundation*.

A great appreciation goes to *Massey's Camera Shop* in Merchant Square for their last minute professional help in this endeavor.

WIMMER
COOKBOOKS

ConsolidatedGraphics
1-800-548-2537

DEDICATION

• • • • • • • • • • •

To Terry Carr, my soul mate, my love and forever my partner in life. The patience, understanding, support and love are more than I have ever known. To Casey Carr, my first born, who has brought the light of true pleasure, changed my life in only the best of ways and fulfills my life in every way. To my youngest daughter Kelly, who once made me feel the greatest cook of all by saying, "I don't want to go out to eat, I want Daddy's cooking." Lou Gerhig said he was the luckiest man on the face of the earth. I feel the same, I would not change a thing.

Thank you Terry Carr.

INTRODUCTION

· · · · · · · · · · · · ·

When telling a person close to me that I was thinking of writing a cookbook, he asked, "Are you trying to leave your mark on something?" Without batting an eye, my immediate response was that I had already left my mark on this world with two precious children, Casey and Kelly. My only motivation was that to write a cookbook seemed to be a fitting conclusion to a lifelong food service career as a Chef.

Never being a person of self-adoring state, but still never lacking self-confidence, I felt it to be a neat thing to do. The sharing of recipes, thoughts, concepts and tips that surround some of my favorite recipes from the restaurants I have had the privilege to be apart of.

To begin this adventure, I have always found myself working in seafood restaurants. My early experiences began as a dishwasher in 1975 where I was first introduced to bluefish. The chef prepared it simply with just butter, lemon and capers, but I will never forget it. I thought it was the best thing I had ever eaten. The sparks began to fly. I also learned a valuable lesson that day. The Chef told the cooks, "always feed and take care of your dishwashers and they will take care of you."

In the summer of 1985 I responded to an advertisement for a Sous Chef at Berret's restaurant. I called and scheduled an appointment with Tom Austin, the general partner. Upon arrival for the interview, I was greeted by a very attractive, friendly, but somewhat inquiring hostess. While trying to focus on the upcoming interview, I paid little attention to her personal questions. She later described me as very quiet and shy. A little more than three years later we were married – true story. The first person I ever met at Berret's restaurant. I wish I could say that it was love at first sight, but it took a couple of years, and now it has been almost fourteen years later.

Being an apprentice myself, I have always found it a responsibility and pleasure to sponsor and train apprentices at the restaurants. The title of this book comes from an exchange of options by apprentices during a class on prepared foods. This saying has stuck with me for a few years. As the story goes, during a verbal exchange on the use of convenience foods, one of our apprentices just listened while others praised the use of products not made form scratch. When our apprentice, Michael Kellum, told the class how we still roasted bones and had overnight reductions for Demi-Glace, the class scoffed. After a short while the apprenticeship instructor asked the class, "Do you know why these chefs and restaurants still roast bones and reduce stocks?" The class had no answer. The instructor answered, "Because, class, there is still romance in food."

I have always been fascinated with the history and tradition of food – the introduction of new influences and food upon people, whether it was by conquering nations or through free exchange. While working as an apprentice and going through college I began reading about Isaac Newton, and one saying hit home: "If I have seen farther than others it is because I have stood on the shoulders of greats." To succeed in humility, appreciate the past and be gracious in success. For the future culinarians, I always expressed the obligation to see farther, do better and make change, but never at the expense of where you came from and who took you there.

I have had the fortune over the years to work with many characters. I think we underestimate the influence and fun these people can bring to our days and lives.

I worked with a manager at Berret's restaurant named Bruce Silverman who own day asked me, "What's it like to be you?" He was of course speaking in a mocking tone. At the same time, he also named me the "curmudgeon of Merchant Square." I had to go home and look up curmudgeon that night before I could be fully insulted.

"We are only a collection of ideas and reflections of the people we know." Now, I wrote that, but what a collection I have had the privilege to be around.

Richard Carr C.E.C.
Executive Chef
Berret's Restaurant
River's Inn Restaurant

ACKNOWLEDGMENTS

• • • • • • • • • • • •

Professionally and personally, a great deal of thanks needs to go to *Tom Austin*, general partner of both Berret's and River's Inn Restaurants. We have seen great times, shared sad times, worked through hard times and had each other's back now for eighteen years. Thank you, Tom, for everything.

To *Jennifer Austin*, thank you for all the hard work in the proofing of a majority of these recipes and giving me a lot of encouragement.

Katherine Sikes, thank you for the proofing and recreating of lost files, a future editor in the making.

Brian Hines, chef at River's Inn, for all the help during the photo shoots, your natural creativeness and talent has shown through over the years.

The many chefs I have stood side by side with over the years. The dishes "we danced with," *David Jones, Wes Holland, Patrick Hilton, Tim Cooper, John Kahler* and once again *Brian Hines* and others who influenced dishes.

The warrior chefs I have gone to battle with, especially *Marshall Hughes, Fred Alcorn* and *Randy Warren*. The abilities and fortitude of these key people to keep it together. The "newbies" on board over the last couple of years, *Robert "Maxie" Sneed, Johnathon Lewis, James White* and *James West*.

The ladies of the kitchen, *Phyllis Allen, Maria Strong, Kristie Lafave* and *Myra Jenkins* among others, thank you.

A special thank you goes out to a chef without whose heart, soul, passion and silent professionalism, as well as the phrase, *"there is still romance in food"* comes, *Michael Kellum*. Thank you, Mike, for restoring my confidence in teaching.

Charlie Little at Berret's, for quite a while during the early years it was just you and me, from soup to dessert. To this day some of that still holds true. Thank God, because that is why Berret's is and has the success it still stands on. Godfather to my children, who still believe he is Stuart Little's uncle, thanks would never do, just love.

To the front of house managers at Berret's and River's Inn, *Steve Smith, Connie Boothe, Crystal Kahler,* "For the love of God" *Brian Mahoney, Sherry Spieght,* and *Paul Suplee.* Thank you for sharing a common goal and making it better.

The much overlooked office staff at the restaurants, *Pam Groman* and *Jennifer Austin,* thank you for the great deal of help over the years in so many ways.

How do you thank family? The family at these restaurants grew out of a dream by Tom Austin and was watered and flourished under the work of some very dedicated, talented and hard-working souls. As families go, we have touched thousands of souls over the past eighteen years and watched relationships form and flourish. There is always one home for all those Berret's souls to come to, 199 South Boundary Street, Williamsburg, Virginia.

Going back in time, the help of *Chef's Mark Kimmal, Rolf Tinner, Rolf Herion, Otto Bernett, Heinz Engist* and *Mr. Fulton,* during the apprenticeship years in instruction. The foundation years as they are called.

To my brother *Larry* and his wife *Debbie,* thank you for being there in the roughest of times over the years. *Mom, Dad* and *Dennis,* as you are looking down from heaven, "Look guys I did it."

This may not be the place, time or the forum, but on September 11, 2002, after feeling a day of remembering, reliving, and relfecting, I just sat down and in five minutes all this seemed to flood out of me as I wrote and I cannot keep it to myself. Forgive me but I think it is important.

I CRY ALONE

• • • • • • • • • • • • •

I can't help thinking about September 11, 2001 as a
day in my lifetime that changed the world.

In trying to process this day of tragedy, I try to place
it in relation to other devastating times in my life.

The loss of close family comes to mind, but those anniversary days,
so to speak are historical and although very sad will never repeat
themselves and are losses to myself alone.

What devastates me is this day changed the life of my children.

The safety of our country, our people and who we are, has been violated.

That makes me cry alone at night on September 11, 2002.

In putting my daughter to bed that night the simplest of
explanations was, they don't understand us and we don't understand them.
But when it comes to violence neither side is right.

My only hope is that this day will awaken the world into a better
understanding for the people of all nations and to mark this day as a new beginning
into a more global peaceful, appreciative and respectful world.

I believe it is the responsibility of both beliefs
to say we are not always right but help me understand.

I cry alone for the loss, the change and the fear that
I now feel for my children and my children's, children's, children's.

God Bless the families of the victims of September 11, 2001.

Richard Carr

CONTENTS

• • • • • • • • • • •

APPETIZERS

· · · · · · · · · · · · ·

APPETIZERS

• • • • • • • • • • • •

Flash-Fried Calamari, 13

Steamed Littleneck Clams, 14

Baked Escargot, 15

Baked Top Neck Clams, 16

Fresh Lump Crabmeat, 17

Baked Lobster Soufflé served with Melba Toast, 18

Old Bay Clam Dip, 20

Fresh Oyster and Surry Bacon Stew, 21

Berret's Baked Oysters O.L.P., 22

Baked Oysters River's Inn, 24

"Taphouse Grill" Oysters, 25

Seared, Rare Yellowfin Tuna, 26

Flash-Fried Calamari served with Garlic Bread, Pesto Cream Sauce, Shaved Parmesan Cheese, Tomatoes and Spring Onions

. . . .

YIELD: 6 SERVINGS

INGREDIENTS:

1 quart frying oil or solid shortening (Crisco)

1 cup flour

Salt and pepper

2 tablespoons dry oregano

1 pound cleaned squid tubes, cut into very thin circles (see HINT)

3 tablespoons olive oil

6 slices thick cut French bread

¾ cup Pesto Cream Sauce (see page 195)

¼ cup coarsely shaved Parmesan cheese

½ cup diced fresh Roma tomatoes

¼ cup finely diced spring onions

2 lemons, cut in wedges

> ### HINT
> . . . .
> *A very helpful hint in the cutting of calamari is to freeze the tubes and cut while still semi-frozen.*

PROCEDURE:

In a large saucepan filled no more than half full, heat oil over a medium-high flame until a temperature of 360-degrees is reached. While cooking, the oil will expand, as well be displaced by the breaded calamari. It is very important to not overfill the pan with oil. To be safe, please use a larger than necessary saucepan. The flour for the calamari should simply be tossed with the salt, pepper and dry oregano. Add the cut calamari, sufficiently coating the calamari with the seasoned flour. During frying, it is not necessary to fry all the calamari at once. Do the frying in two or three stages. The cooking time will only be about two minutes. The longer the calamari cooks, the greater the possibility of it becoming tough.

As the calamari is cooking, place the olive oil-rubbed French bread in a preheated 375-degree oven for about four minutes until toasted. The Pesto Cream Sauce should be reheated slowly in a double boiler and now it is time to "Plate-Up." In the center of the plate place the toasted French bread crouton. Next, ladle about two ounces of the cream sauce over the crouton. Top with a generous amount of the fried calamari, then top with the shaved Parmesan cheese, diced fresh Roma tomatoes and spring onions. Serve with lots of lemon wedges.

> ### TOOLS
> . . . .
> *Measuring spoons and cup, cutting board, chef's knife, large saucepan, basket or such to remove fried calamari, large mixing bowl, baking pan, tongs, pastry brush, double boiler, ladle and hand grater.*

Steamed Littleneck Clams
in a Fresh Herb, Tomato and White Wine Broth

. . . .

YIELD: 4 SERVINGS

INGREDIENTS:

1 quart water

2 clam bouillon cubes (may substitute chicken or other seafood bouillon cubes)

3 tablespoons tomato paste

½ cup finely chopped yellow onion

1 tablespoon chopped fresh garlic

2 tablespoons olive oil

1 teaspoon dried basil leaves

2 teaspoons dried oregano leaves

½ teaspoon crushed red pepper flakes

1 tablespoon finely minced anchovy fillet

½ cup dry white wine, your favorite

24 to 32 littleneck clams, shell cleaned well

PROCEDURE:

In a saucepan, bring the water, bouillon and tomato paste to a simmer. In a separate sauté pan, cook the onions and garlic in the olive oil until translucent. Add the dried herbs, crushed red pepper, anchovies and white wine. Let this reduce until about half of its original volume. Remove this reduction from the heat and add to the simmering stock. Continue to cook for about ten minutes until the new stock has been thoroughly accepted. At that time, add the littleneck clams and cook on medium heat until shells open.

These clams can be served as is, as a lunch entrée or as a dinner appetizer in soup bowls over pasta, with garlic bread and shredded Asiago or Parmesan cheese.

TOOLS

. . . .

Two-quart saucepan, cutting board, sauté pan, chef's knife, measuring cups and spoons, wire whisk and wooden spoon.

Baked Escargot in Shiitake Mushroom, Caramelized Onion and Garlic Butter, topped with Creamy Goat Cheese Croutons

YIELD: 6 SERVINGS

INGREDIENTS:

2 tablespoons olive oil

2 tablespoons chopped fine fresh garlic

½ cup finely diced yellow onion

1 pound fresh Shiitake mushrooms, caps only, diced into ½-inch pieces

¾ pound butter (3 sticks), softened

1 tablespoon finely chopped fresh parsley

Dash of Tabasco sauce

24 freshly cooked snails or canned Helix French snails

24 croutons, cut in circles from white bread

6 ounces cream cheese, softened

6 ounces goat cheese, softened

2 tablespoons finely diced green or spring onions

6 sprigs fresh herbs

3 lemons, cut into wedges

PROCEDURE:

In a sauté pan, place the olive oil, chopped garlic, onions and shiitake mushrooms. Cook until the onions start to caramelize (turn brown) and the mushrooms have absorbed all the oil. Set aside and cool. When the mushroom mixture is cooled, place it in a freestanding mixer with the softened butter, chopped parsley and Tabasco sauce. On low speed, blend the mushroom mixture into the butter until thoroughly combined. Do not over-mix or the mushrooms will turn to mush.

The round, croutons should be the same size as the small ramekins (about the size of a half dollar). Toast the croutons in the oven until lightly brown. Remove and set aside. In a food processor, blend the cream and goat cheeses along with the green onions until smooth. Gently top each crouton with the creamy goat cheese mixture and set aside.

To assemble the escargot, take twenty-four ramekins or 3-ounce casserole dishes and spoon a generous tablespoon of the caramelized onion-garlic butter into the bottom of each. Place a snail on top of the butter in each dish and a creamy goat cheese crouton on top of each snail. Bake the escargot in a preheated 375-degree oven for about 8 minutes. Serve with a fresh herb garnish, lemon wedge and cocktail fork.

TOOLS

Measuring spoons and cup, cutting board, chef's knife, sauté pan, wooden spoon, freestanding mixer, two baking pans, food processor and rubber spatula.

Baked Top Neck Clams topped with Shiitake Mushrooms, Prosciutto Ham, Oregano and Asiago Cheese

. . . .

YIELD: 6 SERVINGS

INGREDIENTS:

½ cup olive oil, divided

¾ pound shiitake mushrooms, caps only, thinly sliced

½ teaspoon pureed fresh garlic cloves

1 teaspoon dried crushed red pepper flakes

1 teaspoon dried oregano leaves

¼ pound Prosciutto ham, thinly sliced into small strips

½ pound Asiago cheese, finely shredded

½ cup coarsely ground breadcrumbs

24 freshly shucked top neck clams

PROCEDURE:

In a hot sauté pan, in half of the olive oil, cook the sliced shiitake mushrooms, garlic, crushed red pepper flakes and oregano until the mushrooms are limp. Add the strips of prosciutto ham and stir until thoroughly combined. Remove from heat and pour into a small mixing bowl. Add the remaining olive oil, Asiago cheese and breadcrumbs. Fold the mixture together as the cheese begins to melt and the breadcrumbs bind the mixture together. This will give a stuffing-type texture to the topping. Set aside and let cool to room temperature. Do not refrigerate at this time.

Take the clams on the half shell and generously top with the room temperature mixture. When topping a clam or oyster, seal the edges with the topping to retain all the natural juices of the shellfish.

TOOLS

. . . .

Measuring spoons and cup, cutting board, chef's knife, clam or oyster shucker, mixing bowl, rubber spatula, sauté pan and baking dish.

Bake in a preheated 375-degree oven for approximately ten minutes or until the topping is hot. Remove from oven and serve.

Fresh Lump Crabmeat baked in Small Casseroles Dishes filled with Shaved Asiago Cheese, Fresh Herbs and "Creamy" Eggs, all served with Toasted Dipping Croutons

YIELD: 8 SERVINGS OF 4 EACH

INGREDIENTS:

9 whole eggs
2 cups heavy whipping cream
2 cups half-and-half cream
½ cup sour cream
1 teaspoon finely chopped fresh dill
Pinch of ground cinnamon

1 tablespoon Montreal seasoning
1 teaspoon blackened seasoning
1 pound fresh jumbo lump crabmeat
½ pound shaved Asiago cheese
16 pieces bias-cut French bread, toasted

PROCEDURE:

In a mixing bowl, place the eggs, heavy cream and half-and-half cream. Whip until thoroughly combined. Now add the sour cream, fresh dill, cinnamon and Montreal and blackened seasonings to the egg mixture and once again whip until the sauce is completed.

To assemble the appetizer for cooking, arrange individual 2.5-ounce casserole ramekins on a baking sheet tray. In each casserole dish place a couple pieces of the lump crabmeat. Sprinkle with the shaved Asiago cheese and pour the sauce mix over top until about a half-inch from the top.

In a preheated 375-degree oven, place the appetizer and cook for approximately 12 minutes or until the casseroles begin to puff up and turn a light brown on top. Remove from the oven and serve immediately with the French bread.

TOOLS

Measuring spoons and cup, one-quart mixing bowl, wire whisk, chef's knife, cutting board, two-ounce ladle and baking sheet pan.

Baked Lobster Soufflé served with Melba Toast

. . . .

YIELD: 4 SERVINGS

INGREDIENTS:

1 (1¼-pound) whole lobster
1 large carrot, finely diced
1 bunch celery, leaves removed, finely diced
4 large shallots, finely diced
2 tablespoons olive oil
¼ cup brandy
2 cups water
2 tablespoon tomato paste

¼ cup white wine
Pinch of salt and white pepper
8 tablespoons butter (1 stick)
6 tablespoons flour
4 whole eggs, separated
Nonstick cooking spray
½ cup Hollandaise Sauce (see page 190)
8 Melba toast or toasted long croutons

PROCEDURE:

Place the lobster in a stockpot filled with enough boiling water to cover and cook the lobster for only about 10 minutes. Remove the lobster from the water and place on a paper towel or napkin to drain. After a few minutes, pull the tail shell away from the center of the lobster and disjoint the claws at the joint closest to the center of the body. Allow cooling then removing the meat from the tail, claws and upper arms of the lobster. When cooled, dice lobster meat.

Take the shell, liquids and any other remaining parts of the lobster and place in a stockpot with the carrots, celery, shallots and olive oil. Cook over a medium-high heat until the vegetables become semi-soft. Add the brandy and deglaze the pan, scraping the bottom to get all the flavors involved. Add the 2 cups of water, tomato paste and white wine. Stir and increase the heat to a boil. Cover and reduce heat to a low simmer. Allow this to simmer for about 20 minutes. Taste and adjust the salt and pepper as needed. Stir until thoroughly combined. Remove from heat and strain, discarding the shells and vegetables. Retain the stock.

TOOLS

. . . .

Measuring spoons and cup, cutting board, chef's knife, stockpot, two saucepans, freestanding mixer, rubber spatula, strainer and patience.

Return the stock to a saucepan and bring to medium-high heat. Reduce by about one-quarter. Strain the stock again to remove any other impurities and once again return to the heat on medium. In a separate pan, melt the butter and add the flour to make a loose roux. Add this to the lobster stock and stir until thickened and a boil is returned. Turn off the heat and pour into a mixing bowl, stirring constantly. Slowly add the egg yolks to the thickened lobster stock, stirring constantly until thoroughly mixed.

In a freestanding mixer, place the egg whites and beat on high until a thick white peak is formed. When the whites can whip no higher, turn the mixer off and slowly fold the whipped egg whites into the lobster stock batter. If the whites begin to break down, go slower.

Once the batter is finished, set up 16 three-ounce ramekins or casserole dishes. Spray the insides with cooking spray and fill the dishes halfway with the batter. Place the chopped lobster meat in the casseroles and cover with the remaining batter. Slowly cook the soufflés in a preheated 325-degree oven for about 20 minutes until they are popping up out of the ramekins. The adage about not slamming doors or peeking in on soufflés because they will fall is TRUE! So be patient, let them cook and serve immediately. I recommend topping with Hollandaise Sauce when the air comes out of the soufflé. Serve with Melba toast or long croutons.

Old Bay Clam Dip

. . . .

YIELD: ABOUT 1 PINT

INGREDIENTS:

4 ounces cream cheese, softened

1 tablespoon sour cream

1 cup mayonnaise

1 tablespoon Old Bay seasoning

2 dashes of Worcestershire sauce

Pinch garlic powder

2 tablespoons finely diced fresh chives

2 tablespoon chopped fresh parsley

1 teaspoon salt

Pinch of Colman's dry English mustard

4 ounces fresh chopped littleneck clams, lightly cooked, chilled and diced (see HINT)

HINT

. . . .

Retain as much of the natural liquid from the clams as possible. If fresh chopped clams are not possible, canned are okay.

PROCEDURE:

In a freestanding mixer, on medium-low speed, place the softened cream cheese, sour cream and mayonnaise. Whip until smooth. Continue to whip while adding Old Bay seasoning, Worcestershire sauce, garlic powder, chives, parsley, salt and mustard. Reduce the speed to low and whip until all the dip is thoroughly combined. With a rubber spatula, scrape down the sides and bottom. Fold the chopped clams and all of the liquid into the dip. This may seem to make dip too thin, but dip will thicken as it chills.

Serve in your favorite dipping bowl with chips, crackers or toast.

TOOLS

. . . .

Measuring spoons and cup, cutting board, chef's knife, freestanding mixer and rubber spatula.

Fresh Oyster and Surry Bacon Stew

INGREDIENTS:

1 quart half-and-half cream

2 clam, seafood or chicken bouillon cubes

7 tablespoons butter, divided

5 tablespoons flour

½ pound bacon, fine diced

½ cup finely diced yellow onion

½ cup peeled and finely diced celery

1 teaspoon white pepper

1 cup heavy cream

24 to 32 freshly shucked oysters

1 teaspoon Tabasco sauce or favorite "hot" sauce

PROCEDURE:

In a saucepan, heat the half-and-half cream with the bouillon until just under a boil. In a separate saucepan, melt 6 tablespoons of butter and add the flour to make the roux. Continue to heat and stir the roux until it is smooth and returns to a boil. Then remove the roux from heat, add to the hot cream and whip constantly until the sauce begins to thicken. At first sign of a boil, remove the thickened sauce from heat and transfer to a clean saucepan and set aside.

In a skillet or sauté pan, render the bacon until crispy, making sure the bacon is fully cooked before adding any other ingredients. When the bacon is crispy, keep all the bacon fat in the pan and add the onion, celery and white pepper. Cook the onions and celery until tender and add all the rendered ingredients to the cream sauce. Get every bit of the bacon fat, scraps and goodies from the skillet. Stir the sauce until thoroughly combined and fold in the last tablespoon of butter and the heavy cream. This finishes the sauce.

To finish the appetizer, in a large sauté pan over medium heat, heat the oysters and "hot sauce". As the edges of the oysters begin to curl, add the sauce and reduce the heat to a simmer, stirring constantly until hot and being careful not to overcook the oysters. Turn off the heat. Ladle the oysters evenly into six soup bowls then cover with remaining sauce. A garnish may simply be some additional crispy bacon or fresh chives.

TOOLS

Measuring cups and spoons, one-quart sauce pan, large sauté pan, cutting board, chef's knife, wire whisk and wooden spoon.

Berret's Baked Oysters O.L.P.

. . . .

YIELD: 8 SERVINGS OF 4 EACH

The O.L.P. simply reflects the abbreviation for the partnership which owns Berret's restaurant, Oyster Limited Partnership, O.L.P. The story behind the Baked Oysters O.L.P. comes from the development of Baked Oysters River's Inn. My not wanting the new and spoiled sister restaurant to have the only signature oyster appetizer, I had to develop the same for the mother ship restaurant.

INGREDIENTS:

½ pound your favorite bacon, about four or five slices

1 pound fresh leaf spinach, washed, stems removed and coarsely cut

2 cups whole milk

3 large yellow bell peppers, stems removed, quartered and seeded

2 tablespoons butter, softened

½ pound (2 sleeves) saltine crackers, crushed

32 freshly shucked oysters

1 cup Hollandaise Sauce (see page 190)

PROCEDURE:

For best results, take the four or five slices of bacon and put in the freezer. When frozen, remove and dice until the smallest slices possible. Place the bacon in a sauté pan and cook until it is crispy. By doing this, the bacon fat will be rendered. This is a very good thing. Add the rendered bacon to the coarse cut fresh spinach in a two-quart mixing bowl and toss until thoroughly combined. It is important to scrape and retrieve every drop of the bacon fat from the sauté pan.

In a saucepan, heat the milk and yellow bell pepper to a slow boil. Lower the heat and simmer for about 20 minutes to let as much of the yellow color break down into the milk. Remove the yellow pepper milk from the stove and place in a food processor. Blend until smooth and yellow. Strain the yellow pepper milk to remove any fibers and debris.

In the mixing bowl containing the bacon and spinach, pour the hot yellow pepper milk. Fold in constantly with a rubber spatula until

> ### TOOLS
> . . . .
> *Measuring cups and spoons, food processor, two-quart mixing bowl, rubber spatula, two wire whisks, small saucepan, sauté pan, cutting board and chef's knife.*

thoroughly combined. At this point, add the softened butter and crushed saltine crackers and once again fold in until smooth. Do not overwork this mixture; stop when the mixture is thoroughly combined. Pour into a shallow container and refrigerate.

When topping is cool, place a generous spoonful on top of each oyster. Be sure to completely cover the entire oyster to seal in all the juices. Bake the oysters in a preheated 375-degree oven for about 8 minutes. When ready to serve, top with a spoonful of Hollandaise Sauce and garnish with some lemon wedges.

Baked Oysters River's Inn

When the opportunity arose to open River's Inn, I wanted to have a signature oyster appetizer. My thoughts were to have a classic scalloped oyster-type recipe but put it on the half shell. To use Virginia products, of course, crabmeat, country ham and seasonings close to home, finished a now very popular appetizer at the restaurant.

INGREDIENTS:

1 pint whole milk

2 tablespoons butter

½ pound (2 sleeves) saltine crackers

2 ounces claw crabmeat, picked and shell-free

1 teaspoon Old Bay seasoning

¼ cup country ham, shredded in a food processor

24 fresh shucked oysters on the half shell

6 ounces Hollandaise Sauce (see page 190)

PROCEDURE:

In a saucepan over medium heat, place the milk and butter and cook until the butter is melted and milk is hot. Do not let come to a boil! In a mixing bowl, place the saltine crackers, crabmeat, Old Bay seasoning and shredded country ham. Hand-crush the saltines into the mixture. Next, slowly add the hot milk to the saltine mixture and with a rubber spatula or wooden spoon fold the ingredients together. Place the dressing in the refrigerator until cool.

When the dressing is cooled, spoon the mixture on the top of the fresh oysters on the half shell. It is important not only to cover the oyster but to seal all around the edges of the oyster with the dressing. This will seal all the oyster liquids during cooking into the dressing. In a preheated 375-degree oven place the topped oysters and bake for about 8 minutes, or until the topping begins to bubble. Remove the baked oysters from the oven and, when ready to serve, top each oyster with a spoonful Hollandaise Sauce and serve with a fresh lemon.

TOOLS

. . . .

Measuring cups and spoons, one-quart saucepan, two-quart mixing bowl, wire whisk, rubber spatula, wooden spoon and oyster shucker.

"Taphouse Grill" Oysters

YIELD: 6 SERVINGS OF 4 EACH

Once again the opportunity to have a signature oyster appetizer for the new outdoor restaurant at Berret's called the Taphouse Grill. Now it is 2002 and the oyster needs a new song. Here it is, a soft topping made with fresh spinach, cream cheese, walnuts and crabmeat, sizzled in a hot oven, topped with crispy locally-smoked bacon.

INGREDIENTS:

1 cup fresh spinach leaves, stems removed and cut into strips

¼ pound special crabmeat, picked clean

4 ounces cream cheese, softened

1 cup walnut pieces or halves

¾ cup sour cream

½ teaspoon Montreal seasoning

½ cup breadcrumbs

24 freshly-shucked oysters on the half shell

24 bacon strips, about two inches each, to top the oysters

PROCEDURE:

Place the cut spinach in a mixing bowl. Flake the crabmeat into the spinach and toss until thoroughly combined. In the food processor, place the softened cream cheese, walnut halves or pieces and sour cream. Process until blended and smooth. Add the Montreal seasoning to the cream cheese mixture and blend again until smooth. Pour the blended cream cheese mixture over the top of the spinach-crabmeat mixture and mix until thoroughly combined. Lastly, fold the breadcrumbs into the mixture to tighten up the topping.

Now take the fresh oysters on the half shell and cover with the creamy topping, making sure to seal the oyster corners. When ready to bake, top each with a slice of bacon. Bake on a cookie sheet in a preheated 375-degree oven for about 8 minutes or until the bacon is crisp. Serve immediately with a fork and lemon.

TOOLS

Mixing bowl, cutting board, chef's knife, measuring cups and spoons, food processor, rubber spatula, medium-sized spoon and cookie sheet.

Seared, Rare Yellowfin Tuna on a Rice Cracker with Sesame Seaweed and "Hot" Wasabi Sauce

. . . .

YIELD: 8 SERVINGS OF 4 EACH

INGREDIENTS: *(for the Tuna)*

- 1 pound center-cut tuna loin, ask for number 1 Sushi quality
- 1 tablespoon cracked black pepper

- 1 tablespoon sea salt, if available, or substitute Kosher salt
- 2 tablespoons olive oil
- 32 rice crackers

PROCEDURE:

Season the tuna loin with the cracked pepper and salt. In a very hot cast iron skillet or sauté pan, place the olive oil. Let the oil settle in the pan. Lower the heat to a medium setting and place the tuna loin in the hot oil. The oil will sear the loin. Rotate the loin around so all sides are seared. Remove from the heat and set aside.

INGREDIENTS: *(for the Sesame Seaweed)*

- 2 cups rinsed, cleaned and hand-dried seaweed
- ¼ cup rice wine vinegar

- 1 tablespoon black sesame seeds
- 1 teaspoon sesame oil

PROCEDURE:

In a saucepan place the seaweed and rice wine vinegar. Cook the seaweed over a medium-low heat until the seaweed has absorbed the vinegar and is limp in texture. Remove from heat and add the sesame seeds and oil and mix thoroughly. Set aside until time to "Plate Up".

INGREDIENTS: *(for the Wasabi Sauce)*

- 1 tablespoon dried or paste Wasabi horseradish

- 1 teaspoon Colman's dry English mustard
- ¼ cup beer
- 1 tablespoon sour cream

PROCEDURE:

In a mixing bowl, combine all the ingredients and mix thoroughly. Taste, if it is too hot, add more sour cream.

To assemble, take the seared tuna and cut against the grain into very thin cracker-sized slices. Place the thinly sliced tuna on a rice cracker. Top with the sesame seaweed and the wasabi sauce. Serve and enjoy!

> ### TOOLS
> . . . .
> *Measuring spoons and cup, cutting board, chef's knife, cast iron skillet, two-quart saucepan, tongs, metal spatula, mixing bowl and wire whisk.*

SOUPS

SOUPS

Chilled Potato and Leek Soup, 29

Chilled Gazpacho with Crabmeat and Fried Tortilla Chips, 30

Fresh Kale, Country Ham and Soft-Shell Crab Soup, 31

Shiitake Mushroom, Country Ham and Leek Soup, 32

New England-Style Clam Chowder, 33

"She" Crab Soup, 36

Watercress and Crabmeat Soup, 37

Spinach and Oyster Soup, 40

Virginia Peanut and Country Ham Soup, 41

Shrimp Bisque, 44

Chilled Potato and Leek Soup

YIELD: 8 SERVINGS

INGREDIENTS:

1 leek, white only, split lengthwise and cut
    into half moons
½ yellow onion, dice fine
1 tablespoon olive oil
3 cups peeled and sliced potatoes
    (about 1½ pounds)

6 cups chicken stock
1 cup half-and-half cream
Salt and white pepper to taste
¼ cup thinly-sliced fresh chives, for garnish
¼ cup crispy bacon bits (optional)

PROCEDURE:

In a four-quart saucepan, place the leeks, onions and olive oil. Cook over a medium heat until the onions begin to turn clear. Add the potatoes and chicken stock. Continue cooking until the potatoes are tender. Remove the cooked potato mixture and let cool at room temperature for about 10 minutes. Place the cooked potato mixture in a food processor or blender and blend on a medium-low speed until completely smooth. Slowly add the half-and-half cream to the mixture and whisk until cream is completely incorporated.

Remove from the food processor and add the salt and pepper to taste. Place in refrigerate for at least 2 hours before service. Taste again after chilling to see if more salt or pepper is needed. Garnish with the fresh chives or crispy bacon and serve.

TOOLS

Measuring spoons and cup, cutting board, chef's knife, four-quart saucepan, wooden spoon, food processor, whip, rubber spatula and ladle.

Chilled Gazpacho with Crabmeat and Fried Tortilla Chips

. . . .

YIELD: 8 SERVINGS

INGREDIENTS:

1 tablespoon blended olive oil

½ cup finely diced yellow onion

1 teaspoon puréed fresh garlic

3 large cucumbers, peeled, seeded and finely diced (about three cups)

½ cup finely diced green bell pepper

3 cups finely diced Roma tomatoes

¾ cup V-8 juice

¾ cup tomato juice

Dash of Worcestershire sauce

Salt and pepper

¼ pound fresh claw crabmeat, picked free of shells

1 cup fried tortilla chips

PROCEDURE:

Place the blended olive oil, onions and garlic in a sauté pan. Cook over a medium heat until the onions begin to turn brown. Remove from the heat and cool. In a food processor, place the cucumbers, peppers, tomatoes and cooled onion mixture. Blend until smooth and pour into a large mixing bowl. Add the V-8 juice, tomato juice and Worcestershire sauce and stir until thoroughly combined. Let the soup cool until time of service. Taste the soup and add the salt and pepper to the level desired. Stir in the crabmeat. Place in a serving bowl and top with the fried tortilla chips.

The soup garnish may vary. More crabmeat, fresh tomato, croutons or even fried soft-shell crab may be used. The soup can be made spicier by adding Tabasco sauce or cayenne pepper.

TOOLS

. . . .

Sauté pan, wire whisk, measuring spoons and cup, cutting board, chef's knife, wooden spoon, food processor, mixing bowl and ladle.

Fresh Kale, Country Ham and Soft-Shell Crab Soup

. . . .

INGREDIENTS: *(for Soup)*

6 cups chicken stock

½ cup finely diced celery

½ cup finely diced yellow onion

6 tablespoons butter

5 tablespoons flour

¼ teaspoon fresh ground nutmeg

½ teaspoon salt

½ teaspoon white pepper

1 pound fresh kale, washed, stems removed and cut into fine strips

¼ cup shredded country ham

INGREDIENTS: *(for Soft-Shell Crab Garnish)*

8 tablespoons margarine (1 stick)

8 "prime" soft-shell crabs, cleaned

Pinch of salt and pepper

½ cup flour

4 tablespoons unsalted butter

PROCEDURE:

In a saucepan, bring the chicken stock, celery and onions to a boil. Reduce the heat to a simmer. In a separate pan, melt the butter and add the flour to make a roux. Cook the roux over a low heat until smooth. Next, add the smooth roux to the slow boil of chicken stock and whisk constantly until the stock begins to thicken. When the thickened stock returns to a boil, remove from the heat. Season the soup with nutmeg, salt and white pepper. Add the cut kale and country ham, stirring until thoroughly combined. Taste the soup again to see if the seasoning needs adjusting. Add more pepper, salt or nutmeg, if desired.

In a sauté pan, melt the margarine over a medium heat. Take the cleaned soft-shell crabs and sprinkle with the salt, pepper and flour. Place the crabs in the hot melted margarine, top shell down. The crabs will begin to brown in a minute or two. Turn the crabs over and finish cooking for about three minutes. Lastly, add the softened, unsalted butter to the crabs and reduce heat. This will add a buttery flavor to the finished crabs. Remove the crabs from the sauté pan and place on a napkin-lined plate at room temperature.

To Plate-Up," pour about eight ounces of soup into a bowl. Take the soft-shell crab and cut directly in half. Place the fried soft-shell crab halves at either end of the bowl and garnish the center with croutons or diced fresh tomatoes.

TOOLS

. . . .

Measuring spoons and cup, cutting board and chef's knife, two saucepans, sauté pan, two wire whisks and wooden spoon.

Shiitake Mushroom, Country Ham and Leek Soup

· ·

YIELD: 8 SERVINGS

INGREDIENTS:

6 cups chicken stock

6 tablespoons butter

5 tablespoons flour

¼ pound shiitake mushrooms caps, stems removed and sliced

1 leek, white only, rinsed, split lengthwise and cut in half moons

¼ cup olive oil

1 tablespoon fresh garlic clove, hand-chopped

1 tablespoon fresh shallots, hand-chopped

2 tablespoons finely chopped fresh thyme leaves

¼ cup country ham, shredded in a food processor

1 teaspoon white pepper

PROCEDURE:

In a three-quart saucepan, bring the chicken stock to a boil. Remove from heat and pour through a fine strainer or cheesecloth to remove any debris from the stock. Return the strained stock to the saucepan and return to a low boil. In a separate saucepan, melt the butter and add the flour to make the roux. Whisk the roux over a medium heat until smooth and cooked. Remove from heat and set aside for a minute to cool slightly. After a minute or two, add the cooked roux to the low boiling stock. Turn the heat up to medium and whisk until the stock begins to slightly thicken and just reaches a boil. At the sign of first boil, turn off the heat.

In a sauté pan, place the mushrooms, leeks, olive oil, fresh chopped garlic, shallots and thyme. Cook until the mushrooms have absorbed all the oil. Pour the cooked mushroom mixture into the thickened chicken stock and gently stir until the soup has incorporated the mixture. At this point, stir in the shredded ham and white pepper and taste. This soup should not need any additional salt because of the country ham and chicken stock.

Garnishes for this soup could be any one of the main ingredients or croutons.

TOOLS

· · · · · · · · · · · · ·

Measuring spoons and cup, cutting board, chef's knife, three-quart saucepan, smaller saucepan, sauté pan, food processor, two wire whisks and ladle.

New England-Style Clam Chowder

YIELD: 12 SERVINGS

INGREDIENTS:

½ pound bacon (your favorite), finely diced (see HINT)

2 cups finely diced celery

1 cup finely diced yellow onion

1 cup finely diced carrots

2 tablespoons dried thyme leaves

5 cups canned or fresh clam juice

3 cups chopped fresh clams, with the liquid (see HINT)

3 cups cooked, diced potatoes, drained

¾ pound butter (3 sticks)

1¼ cups flour

4 cups whole milk

1 tablespoon salt

2 tablespoons white pepper

HINTS

If fresh clams are not available, substitution of cooked, canned clams is acceptable.

To make bacon easier to dice, place the bacon in freezer until fairly solid. "To render" bacon simply means to cook bacon all the way until crispy and until all the fat from the meat has been released.

PROCEDURE:

To start, after the bacon has been rendered down over a medium heat in a small stockpot, add the celery, onions, carrots and thyme leaves. Stir until the onions are translucent (this will take just a minute or two). Next, add the clam juice, fresh chopped clams and cooked diced potatoes.

In a separate pan, heat the butter until melted and add the flour, stirring constantly until smooth. This is the roux or thickening agent for the chowder.

When the clam stock and vegetables come to a boil, it is time to add the roux. The roux should be added rather quickly and the stock should be whisked constantly in order to incorporate the thickening agent. While whisking, the stock will begin to thicken and as soon as the first signs of a boil return to the thickened stock, remove from the heat. Continue to stir the thickened chowder so the bottom does not stick. In a separate pan, heat the milk to just above room temperature and add slowly to the thickened chowder.

It is now time to add the salt and pepper. Taste to see if any additional salt or pepper is needed.

When serving, ladle a generous amount into your bowl and garnish with a choice of additional bacon, cooked corn, carrots, croutons or your favorite garnishes.

TOOLS

Small stockpot, wire whisk, wooden spoon, measuring cups and spoons, cutting boards, chef's knife and two 2-quart saucepans.

Person's Esso Station, Volunteer Fire Department in 1937

One of the first, if not first, "Automatic" Carwash in 1956. In the front right bay of the Esso Station, notice the spray nozzles, lack of brushes and the ceiling fan as the dryer.

Person's Esso Station as seen from the corner of
South Henry and South Boundary, where Berret's Restaurant stands today.

"She" Crab Soup

The amount of "She" crab soup served at the restaurants is mind-boggling. On the average more than one hundred gallons of this traditional creamy crab soup will be served in one week. In addition to the amount of the soup made, more remarkable is that it is made only in five-gallon batches - the way the recipe was originally generated. To make larger batches always compromised the integrity of the soup. Remember it cannot be called "She" crab soup unless it contains the roe of the blue crab.

INGREDIENTS:

1 cup coarsely chopped yellow onion
1 cup coarsely chopped celery
½ gallon whole milk
6 ounces blue crab roe, picked clean
½ pound butter (2 sticks)
¾ cup plus 2 tablespoons flour

¼ pound fresh special crabmeat, picked through and shells removed
½ cup sherry or brandy
1 teaspoon salt
½ teaspoon white pepper

PROCEDURE:

In a food processor, place the cleaned and coarsely chopped onions and celery. Purée until smooth and then strain as much of the liquid out of the puréed mixture. In a saucepan, heat the milk and puréed onions and celery, along with the crab roe, until the milk reaches a low boil.

In a separate pan, melt the butter and add the flour to make your roux. Stir the roux over a low heat until smooth then remove from heat. Add the smooth roux to the low boiling milk mixture and stir constantly until the milk begins to thicken and return to a boil. At the first sign of a boil, remove the pan from the heat and continue to stir until smooth and thick.

You have now successfully made the base for She-Crab soup. It is time to add the crabmeat, sherry, salt and pepper.

TOOLS

Measuring cups and spoons, cutting board, chef's knife, food processor, one large saucepan, two smaller saucepans, and two wire whips.

Let cool for just a few minutes before serving to absorb the flavors of the crab. Taste to see if the soup needs a little more salt, pepper, sherry or whatever you like. By heating a little half-and-half cream and adding it to the finished She-Crab soup, it will give it a thinner consistency. A garnish of some additional crabmeat, thinly sliced spring onion or croutons on top of the soup would be nice and a side of sherry should be poured into the soup at time of service.

When reheating the She-Crab soup, a double boiler is recommended in order to reheat slowly and not scorch the soup.

Watercress and Crabmeat Soup

. . . .

YIELD: 8 TO 10 SERVINGS

INGREDIENTS:

6 cups chicken stock
½ cup finely diced celery
½ cup finely diced yellow onion
8 tablespoons butter (one stick)
6 tablespoons flour
¼ teaspoon nutmeg
2 tablespoons dry sherry

2 large bunches watercress, stems removed and coarsely-chopped
½ pound fresh crabmeat, claw or special meat, picked free of shell
½ cup half-and-half cream
Pinch of salt and white pepper

PROCEDURE:

In a large saucepan, place the chicken stock, celery and onions. Bring to a low boil until the vegetables are cooked. In a separate pan, melt the butter and add the flour to make a roux. Cook over a low heat until the roux is smooth and remove from heat. Next, add the cooked, smooth roux to the low boiling vegetable and chicken stock. Cook and stir until the stock begins to thicken. As the first sign of a boil returns, turn the heat off of the thickened stock and add the nutmeg, sherry and watercress. Stir this until thoroughly combined then add the crabmeat, cream and pinch of salt and white pepper. At this point taste a spoonful of soup and see if it needs a little more salt, pepper or nutmeg. Readjust the seasoning, as you desire.

Serve the soup and garnish with a variety of choices: more crabmeat, fresh tomatoes, croutons or even fried soft-shell crab.

TOOLS

. . . .

Six-quart saucepan or stockpot, a smaller saucepan, wire whisk, measuring spoons and cup, cutting board, chef's knife and ladle.

Virginia Peanut
and Country Ham Soup
see recipe on
page 41

"She" Crab Soup
see recipe on
page 36

Oyster Sampling

Berret's Baked Oysters O.L.P.
see recipe on page 22

Baked Oysters River's Inn
see recipe on page 24

"Taphouse Grill" Oysters
see recipe on page 25

Spinach and Oyster Soup

· · · · · · · · · · · · · · · · · · · ·

YIELD: 8 TO 12 SERVINGS

INGREDIENTS:

1 pint freshly shucked oysters, the smaller
the better for this recipe

1 tablespoon Old Bay seasoning

6 cups chicken stock

½ cup finely diced celery

½ cup finely diced yellow onion

8 tablespoons butter (1 stick)

7 tablespoons flour

½ teaspoon allspice

1 pound fresh spinach leaves, washed, stems
removed and finely-chopped

½ cup half-and-half cream

Pinch of salt and white pepper

PROCEDURES:

In a small saucepan, place the freshly shucked oysters, their liquid and the Old Bay seasoning over a medium heat and lightly poach the oysters until they begin to curl up on the sides. Do not overcook because the oysters are going to receive additional cooking time. Let the oysters cool on a cookie tray with sides.

Reserve all the liquids in a separate pan to add to the soup when needed. When the oysters are cooled, coarsely chop them. Be gentle, it is not important for them to be a uniform size. Set aside.

In a large saucepan, place the chicken stock, celery and onions. Bring to a low boil until the vegetables are cooked. In a separate pan, melt the butter and add the flour to make the roux. Cook over a low heat until the roux is smooth and remove from heat. Next, add the cooked, smooth roux to the low boiling vegetable and chicken stock. Cook and stir until the stock begins to thicken. As the first sign of a boil returns, turn the heat off and add the allspice and fresh spinach. Stir this until thoroughly combined, then add the cooked oysters, the reserved liquid, cream and pinch of salt and white pepper. At this point, taste a spoonful of soup and see if it needs a little more salt, pepper or allspice. Readjust the seasoning as you desire.

TOOLS

· · · · · · · · · · · ·

Six-quart saucepan or stockpot, two smaller saucepans, cookie tray, wire whisk, measuring spoons and cup, cutting board, chef's knife and ladle.

Serve the soup and garnish with a variety of choices: a fried oyster, fresh tomatoes or seasoned croutons.

Virginia Peanut and Country Ham Soup

. . . .

YIELD: 8 SERVINGS

INGREDIENTS:

6 cups chicken stock (see HINT)
½ cup finely diced celery
½ cup finely diced onion
6 tablespoons butter
5 tablespoons flour
1 cup creamy peanut butter
¼ cup shredded country ham (about ¼ pound)

1 tablespoon white pepper
½ cup whole milk

HINT
. . . .
If chicken stock is unavailable, water and bouillon cubes can be substituted.

PROCEDURE:

In a saucepan, heat the chicken stock, celery and onions to a low boil. In a separate saucepan, melt the butter and flour. Stir and cook over a low heat until the roux is smooth. Add the cooked roux to the low boiling chicken stock and increase the heat to medium-high. Stir the thickening stock until it reaches a low boil and turn the heat off. Next, add the peanut butter, shredded ham, white pepper and milk. Stir this until the peanut butter is dissolved and the ham is dispersed throughout the soup. Taste to see if enough salt and pepper has been added. Readjust if needed.

A great garnish is chopped peanuts. An accompaniment of ham biscuits and apple fritters is very Virginia.

TOOLS
. . . .
Measuring spoons and cup, cutting board and chef's knife, two saucepans wire whisk and rubber spatula.

For over a dozen years at Berret's Restaurant in Williamsburg
and seven years at River's Inn, the annual running of the crabs is held.
On Labor Day consecutive weekends the races are held to raise
money for the "Save the Bay" foundation and for the
Gloucester High School Culinary Arts program.

An oyster eating contest
in the late 1980's was
another exciting
fund raiser at
Berret's Restaurant to
raise money for the local
Big Brother-
Big Sister Program.

Shrimp Bisque

. . . .

YIELD: 8 SERVINGS

INGREDIENTS:

6 tablespoons butter

5 tablespoons flour

¼ teaspoon ground red pepper or cayenne

Pinch of ground cloves

2 tablespoon paprika

½ cup finely diced celery

½ cup finely diced yellow onion

¼ pound small shrimp, peeled and deveined

3 tablespoons tomato paste

4 cups seafood stock (see HINT)

1 tablespoon brandy (optional)

1 tablespoon whiskey (optional)

Salt and white pepper to taste

HINT

. . . .

The substitution of chicken stock for the seafood stock is acceptable, or use seafood or chicken bouillon cubes and water.

PROCEDURE:

In a large saucepan over medium heat, melt the butter. Add the flour, ground red pepper, clove and paprika and stir until thoroughly combined and smooth. Reduce the heat to low and add the celery, onion and shrimp. Stir until the vegetables and shrimp are starting to take color. At this time, add the tomato paste and stock and increase the heat to medium-high. Stir until starting to thicken. Continue to stir until the first sign of a boil. At that point, turn the heat off and taste. It is time to add the brandy and whiskey, if desired, and the salt and white pepper to taste.

The garnish to this soup could be additional shrimp, spicy croutons, spring onions, puff pastry or other treats. This depends on the theme, time of year or even occasion at which the soup is served. At a luncheon school function it was garnished with goldfish crackers.

TOOLS

. . . .

Measuring spoons and cup, cutting board and chef's knife, four-quart saucepan or stockpot, wire whisk and serving ladle.

SALAD ENTRÉES
& DRESSINGS
. . . .

**Garlic-Peppered Yellowfin Tuna Steak
served over Boston Bibb Lettuce with
Caramelized Onion-Raspberry Vinaigrette Dressing,
Tomatoes, Fresh Asparagus, Cheddar and Havarti
Cheeses and Roasted Red Bliss Potatoes**
see recipe on
page 66

Rosemary Skewered Sea Scallops
and Grilled Surry Sausage served over a
Fresh Spinach Salad with Warm Honey-French
Dressing, Roasted Yukon Gold Potatoes,
Tomatoes and Sweet Onions
see recipe on
page 62

SALAD ENTRÉES
& DRESSINGS

· · · · · · · · · · ·

House Herb Balsamic Vinaigrette Dressing, 49

Cajun-Spiced Sea Scallops, 50

Roasted Garlic and Bleu Cheese Dressing, 51

Grilled Flank Steak, 52

Barbecue Vinaigrette Dressing, 53

Sautéed Monkfish "Schnitzel", 54

Pommery Mustard and Surry Bacon Vinaigrette Dressing, 55

Flash-Fried Oysters, 56

Caesar Salad Dressing, 57

Pecan-Crusted Chicken Breasts, 58

Mimosa Vinaigrette Dressing, 59

Grilled Crabmeat Salad and Pepper Jack Cheese Quesadilla, 60

Cilantro Sour Cream Dressing, 61

Rosemary Skewered Sea Scallops and Grilled Surry Sausage, 62

Warm Honey French Dressing, 63

Sesame-Crusted Salmon Fillet, 64

Apricot-Ginger Dressing, 65

Garlic-Peppered Yellowfin Tuna Steak, 66

Caramelized Onion and Raspberry Vinaigrette Dressing, 67

Warm Crabmeat, Spinach and Bleu Cheese Quiche, 68

Honey Mustard Dressing, 70

Tarragon-Radish Sour Cream Dressing, 71

House Herb Balsamic Vinaigrette Dressing

. . . .

YIELD: ABOUT 1 QUART

The house dressing for both Berret's and River's Inn Restaurants began a project. I truly wanted a vinaigrette that could compliment and refresh any entrée selection. The selection of aged balsamic vinegar was easy. The compliment of apple cider vinegar, herbs and dissolved sugar adds the lighter, more refreshing side. Lastly, the use of salad oil, not olive oil, allowed the dressing to take on a not clingy or heavy finish.

INGREDIENTS: *(for the Vinegar Mixture)*

½ cup apple cider vinegar
½ cup aged balsamic vinegar
¼ cup sugar
2 tablespoons dried thyme leaves

2 tablespoons dried basil leaves
¼ cup finely chopped shallots
1 tablespoon finely chopped fresh garlic

PROCEDURE:

In a saucepan, heat the two vinegars, sugar, thyme and basil until the sugar is dissolved. Add the chopped shallots and garlic and place in an ice bath to cool.

INGREDIENTS: *(to Finish the Dressing)*

2 whole eggs or the equivalent pasteurized
  eggs
2 tablespoons coarse ground French mustard
  (Pommery type)
2 tablespoons white wine
½ teaspoon salt

1 teaspoon white pepper
Vinegar mixture
2 cups vegetable salad oil
2 tablespoons finely chopped fresh parsley
3 tablespoons finely chopped fresh chives

PROCEDURE:

In a standing mixer, start with the egg, mustard, white wine, salt, pepper and cooled vinegar mixture. Whip at high speed until frothy. Reduce the speed and begin to slowly add the salad oil, adding the oil only as fast as the egg mixture can absorb it. This is the emulsion of the vinaigrette dressing. When emulsion is complete, add the chopped fresh parsley and chives to complete the dressing.

> ## TOOLS
> . . . .
> *Free-standing mixer, measuring spoons and cups, cutting board and chef's knife.*

Cajun-Spiced Sea Scallops served over a Fresh Spinach Salad with Roasted Garlic and Bleu Cheese Dressing, Toasted Pecans, Sweet Peppers, Tomatoes and Tasso Ham

. . . .

YIELD: 6 SERVINGS

INGREDIENTS:

2 pounds fresh sea scallops, 25 count, tag removed

¼ cup Cajun blackening seasoning

Nonstick cooking spray

1½ pounds fresh spinach leaves, stems removed, rinsed and dried

¾ cup Roasted Garlic and Bleu Cheese Dressing

¼ cup toasted pecan pieces

½ cup finely diced red and yellow bell peppers

¼ pound Tasso ham, cut into fine strips

2 vine-ripened tomatoes, cut into wedges

1 loaf crusty French bread

PROCEDURE:

In a mixing bowl, place the sea scallops and the blackening seasoning and toss until thoroughly combined. Place the scallops in a sprayed baking dish in a preheated 375-degree oven for approximately 10 minutes or until the scallops begin to firm up and sizzle. Do not overcook.

To "Plate-Up" the salad entrée, place a generous amount of fresh spinach on the plate and ladle about two ounces of the dressing on the spinach leaves, spreading the dressing around. Set the cooked sea scallops in top of the center of the salad. Sprinkle with the toasted pecans, diced bell peppers and Tasso ham. Arrange the tomato wedges around the plate and served with crusty French bread.

> ### TOOLS
> . . . .
> *Measuring spoons and cup, cutting board, chef's knife, mixing bowl, tongs, baking dish, metal turner and ladle.*

Roasted Garlic and Bleu Cheese Dressing

YIELD: 1 QUART

INGREDIENTS:

¼ cup whole garlic cloves
3 egg yolks
Pinch of salt and white pepper
2 cups salad oil, canola or soybean

2 tablespoons apple cider vinegar
¼ cup water
¼ pound bleu cheese, crumbled

PROCEDURE:

Peel and lightly salt garlic cloves. Roast cloves in a preheated 350-degree oven for about 10 minutes and then cooled. In a food processor, place the cooled roasted garlic and pulse until the garlic is chopped fine. Be sure to retain all the oils and caramelized pieces of the garlic and then set aside.

In the same food processor, place the egg yolks and salt and pepper and whip until smooth and frothy. Slowly add the salad oil until the blend of yolks and oil begins to thicken. This should resemble a mayonnaise. At this point, the vinegar and water should be added to thin out the mayonnaise into a dressing-type consistency. Remove the dressing from the processor into a mixing bowl. Add the crumbled bleu cheese with a spoon and mix thoroughly. If the consistency is too thick, slowly add water. If too thin, slowly add more oil.

TOOLS

Food processor, mixing bowl, cutting board, chef's knife, measuring spoons and cup, wire whisk or wooden spoon.

Grilled Flank Steak served over Fresh Spinach and Radicchio Lettuces with Barbecue-Vinaigrette Dressing, Roasted Yukon Gold Potatoes, Fresh Tomatoes, Sweet Grapes and Flash-Fried Onion Straw

. . . .

YIELD: 6 SERVINGS

INGREDIENTS:

2 cups quartered Yukon gold potatoes
2 tablespoons blended olive oil
Salt and pepper
2 pounds trimmed flank steak
2 tablespoons Montreal seasoning
1½ cups Barbecue Vinaigrette Dressing, divided
1 quart frying oil (Crisco)

1 medium-sized yellow onion, cut into thin rings
½ cup flour
1 pound fresh spinach leaves, stems removed, washed and dried
2 cups radicchio, torn into bite-sized pieces
2 cups vine-ripened tomatoes, cut in wedges
6 clusters red grapes

PROCEDURE:

In a mixing bowl, place the quartered Yukon gold potatoes, blended olive oil and salt and pepper. Toss until potatoes are thoroughly coated and place on a baking pan in a preheated 375-degree oven for about 25 minutes or until fork tender. Remove from oven and set aside.

On a large plate, place the trimmed flank steak. Sprinkle on both sides with the Montreal seasoning and rub with half of the Barbecue-Vinaigrette Dressing. Let set, refrigerated, for about 60 minutes before grilling. On a hot grill, cook the flank steak to the temperature desired (depending upon the grill, about 4 minutes on each side will give you a medium-rare steak). When it is time for service, place the flank steak on a cutting board and cut against the grain of the meat. This cutting method will break down the tendon and give you a tender piece of meat.

TOOLS
. . . .

Measuring spoons and cup, cutting board, chef's knife, large marinating plate, grill, tongs, metal turner, baking pan, rubber spatula, large pot, mixing bowl and ladle.

Fill a large pot no more than halfway with the quart of frying oil and heat on medium-high until the oil is hot (about 350 degrees). If you do not have a high temperature thermometer, take a little water on your finger, drop into the oil, and if the oil starts to pop, then it is hot enough. Dredge the thinly-sliced onions in the flour and carefully drop the onions in the hot oil. Stir and fry until the onions are golden brown. Remove from oil and place on a towel-covered plate.

It is time to "Plate-Up." First, place a generous mixture of the spinach and radicchio in the center of the plate. Next, take the thinly-sliced flank steak and place on top of the greens. Arrange the tomatoes, grapes and roasted Yukon gold potatoes around the lettuces. Drizzle the remaining Barbecue-Vinaigrette Dressing over the salad and top with the flash-fried onion straw.

Barbecue Vinaigrette Dressing

. . . .

YIELD: ABOUT 2 CUPS

INGREDIENTS:

½ cup your favorite barbecue sauce
¼ cup honey
1 tablespoon Worcestershire sauce
1½ tablespoons soy sauce

¼ cup apple cider vinegar
½ cup salad oil, canola or soybean
1 tablespoon Montreal seasoning
Pinch of salt and pepper

PROCEDURE:

In a two-quart mixing bowl, place the barbecue sauce, honey, Worcestershire sauce, soy sauce and cider vinegar. Whisk until smooth.

Slowly add the salad oil and whisk until smooth and until the oil is totally incorporated. Lastly, add the Montreal seasoning and taste, adding more salt and pepper if necessary. Refrigerate until needed but let sit at room temperature before service to let the full flavors restore.

> **TOOLS**
> . . . .
> *Measuring spoons and cup, mixing bowl, whisk and rubber spatula.*

Sautéed Monkfish "Schnitzel" served over Autumn Greens with Pommery Mustard and Surry Bacon Vinaigrette Dressing, Fresh Pears, and Apples

. . . .

YIELD: 4 SERVINGS

INGREDIENTS:

2 whole eggs

1 cup half-and-half cream

2 cups breadcrumbs

1 tablespoon dry oregano leaves

1 tablespoon chopped fresh rosemary

1 tablespoon chopped fresh cilantro

8 (3-ounce) thinly sliced monkfish fillets

¼ cup blended olive oil

1 pound fresh salad greens (your favorites)

1 cup Pommery Mustard and Surry Bacon Vinaigrette Dressing

1 cup peeled and thinly sliced Granny Smith apples (see HINT)

1 cup peeled and thinly sliced pears (see HINT)

HINT

. . . .

Wait until time of service to peel and cut the pears and apples.

PROCEDURE:

In a small mixing bowl, combine the eggs and cream and whip until thoroughly combined. In a separate mixing bowl combine the breadcrumbs and herbs. Dip the monkfish into the egg-cream mixture and then into the herbed breadcrumbs, coating the monkfish thoroughly. Heat the blended olive oil in a sauté pan until hot and cook the monkfish on both sides until golden brown. Remove from the heat and place on a napkin-lined platter to drain any excess oil.

When it is time to "Plate-Up," take the salad greens and arrange in the center of the plate. Next, place the cooked monkfish on top of the salad greens. Drizzle the warm mustard-bacon dressing on the monkfish and salad greens and garnish with the thin slices of apples and pears.

TOOLS

. . . .

Measuring spoons and cups, cutting board, chef's knife, two medium-sized mixing bowls, wire whip, ladle, sauté pan and metal spatula.

A key to the success of this salad is the thinness of the monkish. It should be similar to veal cutlet in the cooking procedure. If the monkfish is thicker, then simply finish cooking in a 350-degree preheated oven until the fish is completely cooked.

Pommery Mustard and
Surry Bacon Vinaigrette Dressing

. . . .

YIELD: ABOUT 1 PINT

INGREDIENTS:

¼ pound Surry or your favorite bacon
  (about 5 slices), finely diced (see HINT)
¼ cup finely diced yellow onion
¼ cup finely diced red bell pepper
1 tablespoon sugar
2 tablespoons coarse ground French mustard
Pinch of salt
1 teaspoon cracked black pepper
¼ cup water

¼ cup white wine or champagne vinegar
1 cup salad vegetable oil

HINT

. . . .

To dice the bacon, place the bacon slices in the freezer until solidly frozen. Freezing the bacon makes it much easier to slice. Slice the bacon as thinly as you can.

PROCEDURE:

Place diced bacon directly into a sauté pan. Cook over a medium heat and stir constantly. When the bacon is crispy and completely cooked, add the diced onion and bell pepper. Stir until the onion is cooked and remove from heat. Add the sugar to the bacon mixture and set aside.

In a free standing mixer, place the mustard, salt, pepper, water, vinegar and the cooked bacon mixture. Blend on medium speed until thoroughly combined. On a medium speed, slowly add the oil until the dressing has completely incorporated the oil.

Now remove the dressing from the processor and place in a small saucepan to heat before serving. This dressing should always to be served warm. The sight of this dressing after refrigerating is not one your cardiologist should see. This dressing does refrigerate wonderfully and just heat or reheat slowly to serve.

TOOLS

. . . .

Measuring cups and spoons, cutting board, chef's knife, medium-sized sauté pan, free standing mixer, rubber spatula, wire whip and ladle.

Flash-Fried Oysters served over a Caesar Salad with Toasted Croutons, Shaved Parmesan Cheese, Tomatoes, Fresh Melon and Strawberries

. . . .

YIELD: 6 SERVINGS

INGREDIENTS:

2 whole extra large eggs

1 pint whole milk

1 tablespoon Old Bay seasoning

36 freshly shucked oysters

1 cup fine ground cracker meal

3 cups solid shortening (Crisco)

2 heads Romaine lettuce, washed and dried

½ cup shaved Parmesan cheese

¾ cup toasted croutons

¾ cup Caesar Salad Dressing

1 vine-ripened tomato, cut into 8 wedges

18 fresh strawberries, rinsed

1 cantaloupe, peeled, seeded and cut into thin slices

PROCEDURE:

In a small mixing bowl, place the eggs, milk and Old Bay seasoning. Whip until thoroughly combined. Gently put the shucked oysters in the egg mixture and set aside. Place the cracker meal in a second mixing bowl. Gently take the oysters out of the egg wash, one at a time, and roll in the cracker meal. Pat the center "yolk" of the oyster and set flat on a wax-lined plate. Refrigerate the breaded oysters, uncovered, for about 15 minutes before frying. In a rimmed fry pan, melt the Crisco and heat until crackling hot. Place a few oysters in the hot oil and fry for about 2 minutes or until golden brown. Remove from the frying pan and place on a paper towel-lined platter to catch any excess oil; set aside. Repeat with all oysters.

In a third larger mixing bowl, place the torn Romaine lettuce, shaved cheese, croutons and dressing. Gently toss until the lettuce is thoroughly coated but not saturated. It is time to "Plate-Up." In the center of the plate, place a generous amount of the dressed Romaine lettuce. Carefully top the salad with six fried oysters. Garnish this non-traditional Caesar salad with four wedges of tomato, three strawberries and some thinly sliced cantaloupe.

TOOLS

. . . .

Measuring spoons and cup, cutting board, chef's knife, three mixing bowls, tongs, rimmed fry pan, large spoon with holes and ladle.

Caesar Salad Dressing

YIELD: ABOUT 1 PINT

INGREDIENTS:

¼ cup pasteurized eggs
   (if unavailable, three egg yolks)
1 teaspoon lemon juice
1 tablespoon Dijon mustard
1 tablespoon finely diced canned anchovy fillets

1 tablespoon finely diced garlic
1 cup salad vegetable oil
Pinch of salt and white pepper
¼ cup apple cider vinegar

PROCEDURE:

In a freestanding mixer on a medium-high speed, place the egg, lemon juice, mustard, anchovy and garlic. Whip until frothy in appearance. Reduce the speed to medium and slowly add the salad oil to the egg mixture. Do not go too fast; allow the egg mixture to completely incorporate into the oil. This is an emulsion, like making mayonnaise. After the oil has been completely absorbed, the dressing will be a little thick. Add the salt and pepper and at a medium speed slowly add the vinegar. This will give the proper consistency and flavor desired.

TOOLS

Measuring spoons and cup, cutting board, chef's knife, freestanding mixer and rubber spatula.

Pecan-Crusted Chicken Breasts served over Mixed Greens with Mimosa Vinaigrette Dressing, Fresh Fruit, Havarti and Cheddar Cheeses

. . . .

YIELD: 4 SERVINGS

INGREDIENTS:

2 cups crushed saltine crackers

½ cup chopped pecan pieces

2 tablespoons flour

2 whole eggs

1 cup whole milk

8 boneless, skinless chicken breasts (about 3 ounces each)

Nonstick cooking spray

1 pound fresh greens, your favorites

½ cantaloupe, peeled, seeded and cut into thin slices

8 fresh strawberries, stems removed and rinsed

8 wedges Havarti cheese

8 wedges sharp Cheddar cheese

½ cup Mimosa Vinaigrette Dressing

½ pint fresh blueberries

PROCEDURE:

In a food processor, place the saltines, pecan pieces and flour. Grind until the breading is smooth and set aside. Next in a small mixing bowl, whip the egg and milk and place the chicken breasts in the mixture to soak. Roll the chicken breasts in the pecan breading until coated and place on a sprayed baking pan. Bake in a preheated 375-degree oven for about 12 minutes.

It's time to "Plate-Up." In the center of the plate, place a generous amount of your favorite greens. Arrange the cantaloupe, strawberries and cheese wedges around the sides of the salad. Place two of the warm pecan-crusted chicken breasts on top of the salad. When ready to serve, drizzle each salad with about two ounces of the Mimosa Dressing and sprinkle with the fresh blueberries.

> ## TOOLS
> . . . .
> *Measuring spoons and cup, cutting board, chef's knife, food processor, two mixing bowls, whisk, baking pan, tongs, metal spatula and ladle.*

Mimosa Vinaigrette Dressing

INGREDIENTS:

1 tablespoon finely diced shallots

1 teaspoon sugar

¼ cup champagne

2 egg yolks
 (pasteurized egg yolks are preferred)

Zest and juice of 1 orange

1½ cups salad vegetable oil

¼ cup champagne vinegar

2 tablespoons honey

PROCEDURE:

In a small sauté pan, heat the diced shallots, sugar and champagne over a low heat until the shallots have caramelized the sugar and absorbed the champagne. The shallots will turn brown and become tender but will not burn. Set aside the caramelized shallots and let cool. In a freestanding mixer, whip the egg yolks and orange zest and juice at a medium-high speed until the mixture begins to show a frothy consistency. Reduce the speed on the mixer to a medium-low and begin to slowly add the salad oil to the frothy egg mixture. Let a slow steady stream of oil fall into the egg mixture until a mayonnaise-type consistency is formed. At this time, still on a medium-low speed, add the champagne vinegar and cooled caramelized shallots to the dressing. Lastly, add the honey to the dressing and whip until thoroughly combined. Refrigerate after service.

TOOLS

Measuring spoons and cup, cutting board and chef's knife, sauté pan, mixer, rubber spatula and zester.

Grilled Crabmeat Salad and Pepper Jack Cheese Quesadilla served over a Mixed Greens Salad with Cilantro Sour Cream Dressing and Charred Tomato and Black Bean Relish

. . . .

YIELD: 6 SERVINGS

INGREDIENTS:

1 pound backfin crabmeat, picked free of shell

¾ cup Imperial Sauce (see page 192)

6 (10-inch) wheat tortilla shells

¾ pound pepper jack cheese, sliced thin

Nonstick cooking spray

1 cup iceberg lettuce, torn to pieces

1 cup red leaf lettuce, torn to pieces

½ pound fresh spinach leaves, picked stem free

1 cup julienne radicchio

1½ cups Cilantro Sour Cream Dressing

1½ cups Charred Tomato and Black Bean Relish (see page 185)

PROCEDURE:

In a mixing bowl, toss the crabmeat and the Imperial Sauce until thoroughly combined. Set out the tortilla shell and place half the cheese on one side of the circle. Top with the crabmeat imperial and again with the remaining cheese. Fold over to create a half-moon quesadilla. When ready to grill, spray a large sauté pan with the cooking spray and, over medium heat, cook the quesadilla on both sides for about one minute or until warm and browned.

In a larger mixing bowl, toss the lettuces, spinach and radicchio together. Place a generous portion in the center of the plates. Drizzle the greens with about half of the Cilantro Sour Cream Dressing. Cut the grilled quesadilla into thirds and arrange on the side of the greens. Garnish the salad with the Charred Tomato and Black Bean Relish and serve the other half of the dressing in a little ramekin for dipping.

TOOLS

. . . .

Measuring spoons and cup, cutting board, chef's knife, two mixing bowls, sauté pan, metal turner, tongs, ladle, large spoon and rubber spatula.

Cilantro Sour Cream Dressing

INGREDIENTS:

1 cup mayonnaise

1¼ cups sour cream

¼ cup fresh lemon juice

1 tablespoon sugar

1 tablespoon onion powder

½ teaspoon garlic powder

½ teaspoon salt

¼ teaspoon white pepper

3 tablespoons finely chopped fresh cilantro

PROCEDURE:

In a large mixing bowl, place the mayonnaise and sour cream, whisking until smooth. Next add the lemon juice and sugar and once again whisk until smooth. Now add the onion and garlic powders, salt, pepper and cilantro and stir until thoroughly combined. This dressing needs to refrigerate for at least an hour to release the flavors of the sour cream and powders.

TOOLS

Medium-sized mixing bowl, wire whisk, measuring spoons and cups, cutting board and favorite chef's knife.

Rosemary Skewered Sea Scallops and Grilled Surry Sausage served over a Fresh Spinach Salad with Warm Honey-French Dressing, Roasted Yukon Gold Potatoes, Tomatoes and Sweet Onions

. . . .

YIELD: 4 SERVINGS

INGREDIENTS:

4 small sized Yukon gold potatoes

Cooking oil

Salt and pepper

1 medium-sized red onion, cut in half then into quarter-inch half moons

4 fresh rosemary sticks, each about six inches long

24 sea scallops, 21 count, washed lightly and tag removed

2 tablespoons olive oil

1 teaspoon Montreal seasoning

4 (3-ounce) smoked Surry sausage links

1 pound fresh spinach leaves, stems removed, rinsed and dried

2 vine-ripened tomatoes, cut into 8 wedges each

1 cup Warm Honey French Dressing

1 loaf warm crusty French bread

PROCEDURE:

Cut each Yukon gold potato into 8 wedges, coat lightly with oil and season with salt and pepper. Lightly oil red onions and place with the potatoes in a preheated 375-degree oven. Cook until the potatoes are fork tender. This should be about 20 minutes. Remove from the oven and set aside at room temperature until time of service.

The rosemary sticks need to be stripped of the actual herb by holding one end and, like a Christmas tree, pull back on the herb against the natural grain. The herb leaves will come right off. Save the herb for another recipe. Skewer 6 scallops onto each rosemary stick. Lightly roll in the olive oil and sprinkle all around with the Montreal seasoning. Place the scallops and sausage links on a hot grill and cook until the

TOOLS

. . . .

Measuring spoons and cup, cutting board, chef's knife, grill, baking pan, tongs and ladle.

Rosemary Skewered Sea Scallops and Grilled Surry Sausage continued

sausage is completely cooked and the scallops are white. (Difficult to give a time for cooking. It depends on the heat of the grill.)

In the center of the plate, place a generous amount of the spinach leaves. Arrange four wedges of tomato, seasoned with salt and pepper, and the roasted potatoes and sweet onions. Next, take the cooked sausage and rosemary skewered scallops and place on top of the spinach salad. Drizzle with about two ounces of the Warm Honey-French Dressing and serve. Some crusty French bread would be a nice accompaniment for a great lunch.

Warm Honey French Dressing

YIELD: ABOUT 1 PINT

INGREDIENTS:

¾ cup chili sauce
½ cup honey
2 tablespoons apple cider vinegar
1 tablespoon sugar
1 tablespoon cracked black pepper

1 tablespoon salt
¼ teaspoon onion powder
¼ teaspoon garlic powder
½ cup salad oil
1 tablespoon finely diced fresh chives

PROCEDURE:

In a two-quart mixing bowl, place the chili sauce, honey, vinegar, sugar and spices and whisk until thoroughly combined. Slowly drizzle the oil into the chili sauce mixture, stirring the entire time to let the oil totally incorporate into the dressing. When the dressing is mixed thoroughly, fold in the fresh chives. To heat, place in a double boiler and heat until just warm before serving over a salad.

TOOLS

Measuring spoons and cup, cutting board, chef's knife, mixing bowl, wire whisk, rubber spatula and a double boiler set-up.

Sesame-Crusted Salmon Fillet served over Napa Cabbage, Baby Bok Choy and Fresh Spinach with Apricot-Ginger Dressing, Cashews, Fresh Tomatoes, Sugar Peas, Matchstick Carrots and Fried Cellophane Noodles

. . . .

YIELD: 6 SERVINGS

INGREDIENTS:

6 (5-ounce) fresh salmon fillets

¼ cup sesame oil

¼ cup white sesame seeds

¼ cup black sesame seeds

Nonstick cooking spray

1 quart frying oil

2 ounces cellophane noodles

1 head Napa cabbage, cut or shredded

1 pound fresh spinach leaves, stems removed, washed and dried

½ cup julienne carrots

½ cup sugar peas

2 cups Apricot-Ginger Dressing

½ cup cashew halves or pieces

½ pint vine-ripened teardrop tomatoes, cut in halves

6 baby bok choy, rinsed and blanched in lightly salted water

Rice crackers

PROCEDURE:

On a large plate, place the salmon fillets and sprinkle on both sides with the sesame oil and the black and white sesame seeds. Refrigerate for about 20 minutes before cooking. On a lightly oiled or sprayed baking pan, place the sesame-crusted salmon fillets and bake in a preheated 375-degree oven for approximately 15 minutes. In a large saucepan, heat the frying oil on medium-high and bring the oil to a 350-degree temperature. If you do not have a thermometer, just drizzle a few drops of water into the oil. If it pops with heat, the oil is ready. Place the cellophane noodles in the hot oil for only about 15 seconds as they will expand and cook very quickly. Remove from the heat and place on a paper-lined platter.

TOOLS

. . . .

Measuring spoons and cup, cutting board, chef's knife, large preparing plate, baking pan, large saucepan, tongs, metal turner, large mixing bowl and ladle.

In a large mixing bowl, add the Napa cabbage, spinach leaves, carrots and sugar peas. Toss until thoroughly mixed and place a generous amount in the center of the serving plates. When ready to serve, ladle two ounces of the Apricot-Ginger Dressing over the greens and place the sesame-crusted salmon on top of the salad. Garnish with the cashews, teardrop tomatoes, lightly-blanched bok choy and a pile of the fried cellophane noodles. Drizzle a little more of the dressing on top of the fish and serve with rice crackers.

Apricot-Ginger Dressing

· ·

YIELD: ABOUT 1 PINT

INGREDIENTS:

3 tablespoons fresh gingerroot, peeled, ground and puréed (see HINT)

1 tablespoon finely diced shallot

¼ cup Oriental duck sauce

1 tablespoon honey

1 cup vegetable salad oil

¼ cup apple cider vinegar

2 teaspoons sesame oil

3 tablespoons soy sauce

2 tablespoons finely chopped fresh cilantro

HINT

· · · · · · · · · · · · ·

If fresh ginger is unavailable, use the ginger in a jar, which is usually pickled. In this case, strain the marinade off of the ginger before using.

PROCEDURE:

In a mixing bowl, place the fresh ginger, shallots, duck sauce and honey and whisk until smooth. Slowly add the vegetable oil, whisking the entire time. This should make a slightly thickened dressing. Slowly add the vinegar, sesame oil and soy sauce to thin out the dressing. Lastly, fold in the fresh cilantro and refrigerate for approximately 30 minutes before serving. This will bring all the flavors together. When ready to serve, let stand at room temperature for a few minutes to get the chill off and let the oils loosen up.

TOOLS

· · · · · · · · · · · · ·

Measuring spoons and cup, cutting board and chef's knife, mixing bowl and whip and rubber spatula.

Garlic-Peppered Yellowfin Tuna Steak served over Boston Bibb Lettuce with Caramelized Onion-Raspberry Vinaigrette Dressing, Tomatoes, Fresh Asparagus, Cheddar and Havarti Cheeses and Roasted Red Bliss Potatoes

YIELD: 6 SERVINGS

INGREDIENTS:

½ pound red bliss potatoes, as small as possible, cut in half

4 tablespoons olive oil, divided

Salt and cracked black pepper

6 (5-ounce) fresh yellowfin tuna steaks

2 tablespoons Montreal seasoning

2 heads fresh Boston Bibb lettuce, washed

1½ cups Caramelized Onion and Raspberry Vinaigrette Dressing

½ pint vine-ripened teardrop tomatoes, cut in half

½ pound fresh asparagus, peeled and lightly blanched in salt water

½ pound sharp Cheddar cheese, cut into wedges

½ pound dill Havarti cheese, cut into wedges

PROCEDURE:

In a mixing bowl toss the cut red bliss potatoes with half of the olive oil, salt and cracked black pepper. Place on a baking pan in a preheated 375-degree oven and cook for about 20 minutes or until fork tender. Remove the potatoes from the oven and set aside.

On a large plate, place the tuna steaks and sprinkle on both sides with the rest of the olive oil and Montreal seasoning. Let set a few minutes before grilling. On a hot grill, place the seasoned tuna steaks and cook for about 3 minutes on each side, depending upon thickness of the steak. Try to serve the tuna between medium-rare and medium. Do not over cook the tuna steak or it will be very dry.

Now let's "Plate-Up." In the center of the plate, place a generous amount of the Boston Bibb lettuce. Set the grilled tuna steak somewhat near the center of the plate. Drizzle the Caramelized Onion-Raspberry Dressing all over the lettuce and tuna. Garnish the plate with the halved teardrop tomatoes, warm red bliss potatoes, lightly-blanched asparagus and wedges of the Cheddar and Havarti cheeses.

> ### TOOLS
>
> *Measuring spoons and cup, cutting board, chef's knife, grill, metal turner, tongs, mixing bowl, baking pan, ladle and large spoon.*

Caramelized Onion and Raspberry Vinaigrette Dressing

YIELD: ABOUT 1 PINT

INGREDIENTS:

1 large red onion, thinly sliced
Pinch of salt and pepper
2 tablespoons sugar
Nonstick cooking spray
½ cup raspberry vinegar

¼ cup pasteurized egg or 2 whole eggs
1 tablespoon Dijon mustard
2 tablespoons honey
1 cup salad vegetable oil

PROCEDURE:

In a mixing bowl, place the thinly sliced red onion, salt, pepper and sugar. Cover and refrigerate for about 24 hours. After about 24 hours, remove the red onion from the mixing bowl without any liquid (the onion will leach out a lot of liquid) and place on a sprayed baking pan. In a preheated 225-degree oven, cook the onions for about 1 hour or until brown and dried.

In a food processor place the dried onion and the raspberry vinegar and purée until smooth. In a freestanding mixer, place the pasteurized egg, mustard and honey and whip on high speed until frothy. Add the puréed onion and vinegar to the egg mixture and whip again until frothy. Now reduce the speed to medium and slowly drizzle the salad oil into the mixer, making sure the oil is being incorporated into the egg mixture. Let mix for a minute or two after the oil is added, until the vinaigrette is finished.

TOOLS

Measuring spoons and cup, cutting board and chef's knife, mixing bowl and whip, rubber spatula, mixing bowl, baking pan and food processor.

Warm Crabmeat, Spinach and Bleu Cheese Quiche served with a Mixed Greens Salad with House Vinaigrette

YIELD: 8 TO 10 SERVINGS

INGREDIENTS: *(for Quiche Filling)*

¼ pound bacon, finely diced

3 tablespoons finely diced shallots

2 tablespoons finely diced garlic

½ pound shiitake mushroom caps, sliced

1 medium-sized red bell pepper, finely diced

1 tablespoon Montreal seasoning, divided

5 tablespoons olive oil, divided

½ pound fresh spinach leaves, washed, stems removed

12 ounces claw crabmeat, picked free of shell

¼ pound bleu cheese, crumbled into small pieces

1 cup breadcrumbs

INGREDIENTS: *(for Custard Filling)*

10 whole eggs

1 quart half-and-half cream

PROCEDURE:

In a large sauté pan, over medium heat, render the bacon. (Render means to cook the bacon until crispy, stirring constantly until all the fat has been released into the pan and a white foam appears.) Don't be tempted to add the other ingredients too quickly because the water from the other ingredients will stop the bacon from completely rendering. With the bacon rendered, add the shallots, garlic, mushrooms, bell pepper, 1 teaspoon of Montreal Seasoning and 3 tablespoons of the olive oil. The amount of olive oil is judgmental with the fat content of the bacon. The main idea is to have enough oil to absorb into the mushrooms and peppers.

TOOLS

Large sauté pan, two large mixing bowls, wooden spoon, measuring cups and spoons, springform pan, cutting board, chef's knife, wire whisk and large ladle.

In a large mixing bowl, place the spinach, crabmeat, two tablespoons of olive oil and the other teaspoon of Montreal Seasoning. Toss together until thoroughly combined. Pour the warm mushroom sauté over the spinach mixture and toss vigorously, wilting the spinach and mixing the other ingredients.

After the mixture has cooled a few minutes, add the crumbled bleu cheese and mix together.

It is time to assemble the quiche. In a springform pan, press the breadcrumbs on the base to form a firm foundation. Next, spray generously the sides and top of the breadcrumbs with cooking spray. The spinach-crabmeat filling should be loosely distributed in the pan.

Beat the eggs and cream of the custard filling together and ladle over the filling. Let settle for at least 15 minutes. Pat the top of the quiche smooth and place in preheated 300-degree oven for about 60 minutes. Rotate the quiche about halfway through the cooking cycle. Do the clean toothpick test after you believe the custard filling is firming up. When finished cooking, let sit at room temperature for at least 20 minutes before refrigerating or serving.

Honey Mustard Dressing

. . . .

YIELD: ABOUT 1 PINT

INGREDIENTS:

½ cup honey
¼ cup Dijon mustard
½ cup yellow mustard

1 cup vegetable salad oil
1 tablespoon celery seeds

PROCEDURE:

In a two-quart mixing bowl, place the honey, Dijon mustard and yellow mustard and whisk until thoroughly combined. Slowly drizzle the oil into the honey-mustard mixture, stirring the entire time to let the oil totally incorporate into the dressing. When the dressing is mixed thoroughly, fold in the celery seeds.

TOOLS

. . . .

Measuring spoons and cup, mixing bowl, wire whisk and rubber spatula.

Tarragon-Radish Sour Cream Dressing

YIELD: ABOUT 1 PINT

INGREDIENTS:

3 tablespoons fresh radishes, ends snipped and puréed

2 tablespoons finely chopped fresh tarragon leaves

3 tablespoon white wine

½ cup mayonnaise

½ cup sour cream

¼ cup half-and-half cream

1 tablespoon sugar

1 tablespoon lemon juice

1 teaspoon onion powder

½ teaspoon garlic powder

½ teaspoon salt

½ teaspoon white pepper

PROCEDURE:

In a small sauté pan, place the puréed radish, tarragon leaves and white wine over a medium-low heat and allow the radish and tarragon to absorb the wine. Remove from the heat and refrigerate the radish mixture until needed later in the recipe. In a mixing bowl, combine the mayonnaise, sour cream, half-and-half cream, sugar and lemon juice, and whisk until a smooth consistency is present. Then add the onion powder, garlic powder, salt and white pepper. Once again, whisk the dressing until the spices are thoroughly incorporated. Add the cooled radish mixture and stir until thoroughly combined. Refrigerate until time of service.

TOOLS

Measuring spoons and cup, cutting board, chef's knife, sauté pan, whisk, rubber spatula and mixing bowl.

SEAFOOD ENTRÉES

SEAFOOD ENTRÉES

• • • • • • • • • • •

Spicy Cornmeal-Crusted Catfish Fillet, 76

Berret's "Traditional" Pan-Fried Crab Cakes, 78

Pan-Fried Lump Crab Cakes, 79

Fresh Flounder Fillet, 80

Flash-Fried Virginia Oysters, 84

Almond and Saltine-Crusted Shrimp, 88

Steamed Whole Maine Lobster, 89

Pecan-Crusted Flounder Fillet, 92

Potato-Crusted Salmon Fillet, 96

Cajun Red Beans and Rice, 98

Fresh Virginia Rockfish, 100

Rosemary-Skewered Sea Scallops, 102

Seared Salmon Fillet, 104

Fresh Sea Scallop, Shrimp, Crawfish and
Littleneck Clam "Étouffée", 106

Fresh Sea Scallops, Shrimp and Lobster, 108

Fresh Shad Roe, 110

Pan-Fried Soft-Shell Crabs, 112

Sautéed Gulf Shrimp and Lump Crabmeat, 114

Grilled Yellowfin Tuna Steak, 115

Baked Crabmeat Imperial between Puff Pastry, 116

"THE DANCE WE DO"

• • • • • • • • • • •

While putting together our seafood dishes, we focus on the prime ingredient as our starting point, then move on to the "theme" or complimentary ingredients needed to surround the prime ingredient. A long time ago while working at Pier 13 in Richmond, I described this to an apprentice as "the dance we do." It usually starts out slow and then, kind of like jazz, the ideas begin triggering other ideas and the next thing you know, a pretty cool spontaneous dish is born.

I once thought of a chapter based on "Salmons of the World." We have done so many presentations with salmon based on a new theme or combining different cultural standards on the same plate.

Back to the dance, it usually begins with the main idea and then it expands into some traditional, or not so traditional, accompaniments – what it goes well with, compliments, tones down, or pulls it all together. This may sound pretty vague, but here would be an example. Main ingredient: Salmon, potato crusting. Okay, so Potato-Crusted Salmon Fillet. Now, what sauce would go well with potato crusting? There are many options, but how about using the potato as the spin-off – a cream sauce made with sour cream and horseradish. So we have Potato-Crusted Salmon Fillet served with Horseradish Cream Sauce. Now we need a theme or something to pull it all together. The potato thing is still the draw, so how about bacon, spring onions, butter, and tomatoes? All the things you love to load on a baked potato, okay, okay.

Potato-Crusted Salmon Fillet
served over Horseradish Cream Sauce and
topped with Sautéed Applewood Bacon
and Fresh Tomatoes in Spring Onion Butter

There a dish or dance is born. It is fun, sometimes you never know where it will end up, sometimes it needs to be reeled in a little, but for the most part, it is kind of like jazz.

Spicy Cornmeal-Crusted Catfish Fillet served with a Cheddar Cheese and Country Ham Grit Cake, Hanover Tomatoes, Fresh Asparagus and Cilantro Sour Cream Dressing

YIELD: 6 SERVINGS

INGREDIENTS:

1 cup buttermilk

2 whole eggs

6 (6-ounce) skinless catfish fillets

1 cup cornmeal

¼ cup flour

1 tablespoon blackened seasoning (Chef Paul's)

½ cup blended olive oil

Nonstick cooking spray

6 Cheese and Ham Grit Cakes (see page 178)

3 large Hanover tomatoes, thickly sliced and chilled

½ pound fresh asparagus, peeled and lightly blanched in salt water

¾ cup Cilantro Sour Cream Dressing (see page 61)

Fresh cilantro for garnish

PROCEDURE:

In a large mixing bowl, whip the buttermilk and eggs together to make an egg wash. Place the catfish fillets in the egg wash to soak for a few minutes. In a rimmed plate, combine the cornmeal, flour and blackened spices and mix until thoroughly combined. Place the wet catfish fillets into the cornmeal mixture and coat the fillets on both sides. In a sauté pan, add the blended olive oil and when hot, place the catfish fillets, three at a time, into the hot oil. Reduce the heat to medium and cook for about 2 minutes on each side.

TOOLS

Measuring spoons and cup, cutting board, chef's knife, large mixing bowl, whisk, large rimmed plate for breading, skillet, metal turner, baking pan, two sauté pans, ladle and tongs.

Remove the catfish fillets from the sauté pan and place on a baking pan sprayed with cooking spray. Place the crusted catfish into a preheated 375-degree oven and bake for about 10 minutes. The cooking time depends on the thickness of the fillets.

Spicy Cornmeal-Crusted Catfish Fillet continued

In a separate sauté pan, sprayed with cooking spray, place the grit cakes and cook over a medium heat for about 2 minutes on each side until crispy. Remove from the pan and place on a paper towel-lined plate to absorb any excess oil.

Now it is time to "Plate-Up." Place a cooked grit cake at about two o'clock from the center of the plate. Next, arrange the chilled, sliced Hanover tomatoes toward the bottom of the plate and set the catfish fillet across the plate, leaning against the grit cake. To garnish the plate, place the warm, blanched asparagus next to the catfish and then drizzle two ounces of the Cilantro Sour Cream Dressing around the plate with a few sprigs of fresh cilantro.

Berret's "Traditional" Pan-Fried Crab Cakes served over Thinly-Sliced Country Ham and topped Sweet Corn Relish, all served with Red Pepper Tartar Sauce

. . . .

YIELD: 4 SERVINGS

INGREDIENTS:

1 whole extra large egg

½ cup mayonnaise

¼ teaspoon Colman's dry English mustard

¼ teaspoon ground white pepper

1 tablespoon chopped fresh parsley

2 dashes of Tabasco sauce

½ pound special or regular crabmeat, picked clean of shell

½ pound claw crabmeat, picked free of shells

2 cups breadcrumbs

½ cup blended olive oil

4 ounces country ham, sliced thin

1 cup Sweet Corn Relish (see page 173)

1 cup "Berret's" Tartar Sauce (see page 201)

PROCEDURE:

In a mixing bowl, combine the egg, mayonnaise, dry mustard, white pepper, chopped parsley, Tabasco sauce and whip until smooth. Gently fold in the crabmeat and toss until thoroughly combined.

To make the crab cakes, gently separate the crab mixture into eight even balls. Take the crab balls and roll them in the breadcrumbs, patting the balls to flatten into natural looking crab cakes. When it is time to cook the crab cakes, place the blended olive oil in a large sauté pan over medium heat. When the oil is hot, place the crab cakes into the hot oil and cook for about 2 to 3 minutes on each side or until browned. Remove the crab cakes from the sauté pan and place on a paper towel-lined plate to absorb any excess oil.

TOOLS

. . . .

Measuring spoons and cup, cutting board, chef's knife, two small mixing bowls, whisk, sauté pan, metal turner, large spoon and ladle.

Now it is time to "Plate-Up." Place the thinly-sliced ham in the center of the plate and lean the cooked crab cakes against each other on top of the ham. Lastly, top the crab cakes with the Sweet Corn Relish and place a generous amount of the tartar sauce in a couple of different spots on the plate.

Pan-Fried Lump Crab Cakes served with Sweet Peppered Green Cabbage Slaw and Rémoulade Sauce

YIELD: 4 SERVINGS

INGREDIENTS:

1 whole egg
½ cup mayonnaise
1 teaspoon Colman's dry English mustard
½ teaspoon ground white pepper
1 tablespoon finely chopped fresh parsley
2 dashes Tabasco sauce

1 pound fresh jumbo lump crabmeat, picked clean
¼ pound fresh special crabmeat, picked clean
2 cups breadcrumbs
½ cup blended olive oil
½ head radicchio lettuce
1½ cups Sweet Pepper Green Cabbage Slaw (see page 184)
1 cup Rémoulade Sauce (see page 200)

PROCEDURE:

In a medium-sized mixing bowl, combine the egg, mayonnaise, dry mustard, pepper, parsley and Tabasco sauce and whip until smooth. Add the crabmeat to the sauce and gently toss until wet. Be very careful to not break up the large lumps of crabmeat. Portion the crab cake mixture into eight relatively even balls. The next step is to roll the portioned balls into the breadcrumbs and flatten gently for cooking purposes.

In a large skillet, heat blended olive oil until hot. Place the crab cakes into the hot skillet and cook for approximately 2 to 3 minutes on each side or until golden brown. Remove the crab cakes from the skillet and place on paper-lined platter to absorb any excess oil.

It is now time to "Plate-Up." Take an outer leaf of the radicchio and form a cup for the slaw. In the center of the plate, place a generous amount of the slaw into the radicchio cup. Turn the cup away from the center of the plate to prevent the vinegar dressing from running into the crab cakes. Place two crabmeat cakes to one side of the slaw and drizzle about two ounces of the Rémoulade Sauce on the other side. Depending upon availability, grilled asparagus, fresh Hanover tomatoes, local walnuts and fresh baked breads would be great accompaniments to a great crab cake.

TOOLS

Measuring cups and spoons, cutting board and chef's knife, two medium-sized mixing bowls, wire whisk, large skillet, metal turner, spatula and tongs.

Fresh Flounder Fillet rolled with Crabmeat Imperial and Thinly-Sliced Prosciutto Ham, served with Béarnaise Sauce and Grilled Summer Vegetables

. . . .

YIELD: 6 SERVINGS

INGREDIENTS:

1 pound backfin crabmeat, picked free of shell

½ cup Imperial Sauce (see page 192)

6 (6-ounce) boneless, skinless flounder fillets

6 (½-ounce) thin slices prosciutto ham

2 tablespoons olive oil

1 tablespoon Montreal seasoning

½ cup Italian breadcrumbs

Nonstick cooking spray

¼ cup white wine

2 tablespoons finely chopped fresh tarragon

1 tablespoon finely diced shallots

1 tablespoon champagne vinegar

¾ cup Hollandaise Sauce (see page 190)

2 cups summer vegetables, cut julienne or big-bite size, squash, bell peppers, sugar peas, asparagus and others

3 tablespoons vegetable oil

Salt and pepper

PROCEDURE:

In a small mixing bowl, place the backfin crabmeat and mix with the Imperial Sauce, gently tossing until thoroughly combined. Next, take the skinless flounder fillets and double check to make sure there are no bones remaining in the fillets. On a smooth surface, lay the fillets flat and place the prosciutto ham down covering the inside of the entire fillet. Now, evenly distribute the crabmeat imperial in the center of the six fillets and roll the fillets around the ball of crabmeat imperial. This will give you six flounder fillets rolled with the prosciutto ham and crabmeat imperial. Sprinkle the flounder rolls with a little olive oil, Montreal seasoning and Italian breadcrumbs. Place the rolled flounder fillets on a sprayed baking dish. Place in a preheated 375-degree oven and bake for approximately 20 minutes, depending on the size of the rolls. When finished baking, the fish should be white in color and the internal ingredients should be hot.

TOOLS

. . . .

Measuring spoons and cup, cutting board, chef's knife, two mixing bowls, baking dish, sauté pan, rubber spatula, metal turner, whisk, tongs and ladle.

Fresh Flounder Fillet continued

In a small sauté pan, place the white wine, fresh tarragon, shallots and champagne vinegar. Cook over a medium heat until the liquids are dissolved into the tarragon and shallots. This is called a tarragon reduction. Let the reduction cool at room temperature then whisk into the Hollandaise sauce to make Béarnaise sauce.

To finish this dish, take the vegetables of your choosing and toss with the vegetable oil, salt and pepper. Grill the vegetables and arrange in the center of the plate. Place the baked flounder roll on top of the grilled vegetables and pour about ¼ cup of the Béarnaise sauce around the fish and the grilled vegetables.

Cajun Red Beans and Rice
with Fresh Sea Scallops, Shrimp,
Littleneck Clams, Smoked Surry Sausage
and Confit Duck Leg
see recipe on page 98

Fresh Shad Roe served with Crisp Bacon,
Tomatoes, Grilled Sweet Onions,
Spring Onions and Poached Eggs
see recipe on
page 110

Flash-Fried Virginia Oysters served over Thinly-Sliced Country Ham with Cheddar Cheese Grits, Baby French Green Beans and Traditional "River's Inn" Tartar Sauce

. . . .

YIELD: 6 SERVINGS

I like to use "count" oysters for frying. The smallest of the shucked oysters packed are called standard. The next size up is selects and then counts. I like a good-sized oyster for the evenness and texture of the finished fried oyster. I judge a very good seafood restaurant by many standards and one is the integrity of their fried oysters. A simple dish that can be done horribly, if the oyster is not treated with the respect the oyster deserves.

"The pearl of a very good seafood restaurant, no pun intended."

INGREDIENTS:

2 whole eggs

2 tablespoons Old Bay seasoning, divided

2 cups whole milk or half-and-half cream

36 to 42 shucked oysters, size called "counts"

2 cups fine ground cracker meal

1 quart vegetable frying oil

½ pound thinly-sliced country ham

6 servings Cheddar Cheese Grits (see page 172)

1 pound baby French green beans, ends snapped and lightly blanched in salted water

1½ cups Traditional "River's Inn" Tartar Sauce (see page 201)

PROCEDURE:

In a large mixing bowl, place the eggs, one tablespoon of Old Bay seasoning and the milk or cream. Whip until thoroughly combined. This is called an egg wash and will help the oyster stick to the breading. Place the oysters in the egg wash and let sit in a refrigerator for a few minutes before breading.

In a casserole dish, mix the cracker meal and the other tablespoon of Old Bay seasoning. Place the wet oysters into the cracker meal, a couple at a time, and gently coat with the

---

TOOLS

. . . .

Measuring spoons and cup, cutting board, chef's knife, large saucepan, spoon with holes, casserole dish, mixing bowl, whip, fryer thermometer, large spoon, ladle and respect for oysters.

seasoned cracker meal. Be very careful with the center or "yolk" of the oyster while breading. After breading, lay the oysters out on a wax paper-lined dish and refrigerate, uncovered. The reason for leaving the oysters uncovered is to let the breading dry out. If the oysters are covered, they will get moist, soggy and very dark during frying.

Fill a large saucepan no more than half full with vegetable frying oil. This is very important; do not fill any cooking vessel that will contain oil more than half full. The oil expands during frying and the introduction of other items into the oil could cause an overflow. If the oil were to overflow onto an open flame while frying, you would be looking for a new address. Heat the oil over a medium-high heat until the oil reaches about 360-degrees. If you do not have a high temperature thermometer, flick a sprinkle of water into the oil and if it crackles, you are ready to fry. When the oil is hot, lower the temperature just a little to medium. If you find the oil becoming sluggish or not crackling during frying, bring the temperature back up.

When frying the oysters, submerge a few at a time into the hot oil and cook each round of the oysters for about two minutes until golden brown. Remove the oysters from the hot oil and place on a paper-lined platter to absorb any excess oil. At that time, you could sprinkle on a little Old Bay seasoning, if desired. Continue frying until all the oysters are golden brown and ready to serve.

Now it is time to "Plate-Up." First, take the thinly-sliced country ham and place at the bottom of the plate. Next, take a generous amount of the cheese grits and place at the ten o'clock spot of the plate. Arrange the lightly-blanched baby green beans against the cheese grits. Pile the fried oysters on top of sliced country ham and serve. In small open side dishes, serve the tartar sauce for dipping.

Early in 1995, the renovation of River's Inn Restaurant
at the York River Yacht Haven in Gloucester Point, Virginia

In May of 1996, the opening of the River's Inn Restaurant

Berret's "Traditional" Pan-Fried Crab Cakes
served over Thinly-Sliced Country Ham and
topped with Sweet Corn Relish, all served
with Red Pepper Tartar Sauce
see recipe on
page 78

Almond and Saltine-Crusted Shrimp

. . . .

YIELD: 4 TO 6 SERVINGS

This crusting can be used in other seafood, such as white fishes, scallops and crab cakes. The cooking methods on these dishes could vary as well, from baked fish to pan-fried.

INGREDIENTS:

2 whole eggs

1 tablespoon almond extract or almond liqueur

2 cups half-and-half cream

½ pound saltine crackers (2 sleeves of the elf's favorite), divided

½ cup sliced blanched almonds, crushed in small pieces

2 cups flour

24 shrimp, 16 count, shell removed, butterflied and deveined

1 quart solid shortening (Crisco)

PROCEDURE:

In a small mixing bowl, combine the egg, almond extract and half-and-half cream. Whip until thoroughly combined. This is called an egg wash. In a food processor, place three quarters of the saltines and grind until smooth. Put the finely ground saltines into a casserole dish. Crush by hand the remaining quarter of the crackers and mix with the finely-ground cracker crumbs. To complete the crusting, add the crushed almonds to the saltine mixture and mix thoroughly. The third element for the breading stations is a container for the flour.

The breading stations are now in place. First, take the butterflied shrimp by the tail and dredge through the flour. Try to keep the tail clean through all stages of the breading process. Dip the floured shrimp into the egg wash mixture and then into the ground saltine-almond breading. Coat the entire shrimp with the almond crusting and set aside. Continue this process until all the shrimp are crusted.

In a fry-daddy or a large saucepan, place the solid shortening, no more than half full, and bring to a medium-high heat. When the oil reaches 360-degrees, lower the heat to medium. If the oil becomes sluggish during frying return the heat to medium-high. Place the shrimp in the hot oil, a few at a time, keep separated and cook for about two minutes or until golden brown. Use a slotted spoon to remove the shrimp from the hot oil onto a paper-lined platter. The paper will absorb any excess oil. Continue this process until all the shrimp are fried. After removing the shrimp from the hot oil, sprinkle with some additional almonds or salt, depending upon your preference. Serve the shrimp with cocktail or Rémoulade sauce.

TOOLS

. . . .

Measuring spoons and cup, mixing bowl, wire whip, large saucepan or fry-daddy, slotted spoon and food processor.

Steamed Whole Maine Lobster filled with Crabmeat Imperial and topped with Toasted Breadcrumbs and Dill Hollandaise Sauce

· ·

YIELD: 6 SERVINGS

INGREDIENTS:

2 gallons water, lightly salted

6 (1½-pound) whole Maine lobsters

1 pound backfin crabmeat, picked free of shell

½ cup Imperial Sauce (see page 192)

2 tablespoons blended olive oil

1 tablespoon Montreal seasoning

½ cup Italian breadcrumbs

2 tablespoons finely chopped fresh dill

¼ cup white wine

1 tablespoon finely diced shallots

1 tablespoon champagne vinegar

¾ cup Hollandaise Sauce (see page 190)

PROCEDURE:

In a large stock pot, bring about 2 gallons of lightly salted water to a rapid boil. Place the lobsters in the water and cook for about eight minutes. The lobsters need not be fully cooked at this point, as they will require additional cooking time. Remove the lobsters from the boiling water and place in a large sink or pan of iced water. This will stop the cooking process and cool the lobsters.

Break the claws and arm meat away from the shell and set aside. Turning the lobster on its back, take a sharp knife and split through the tail and halfway up the upper body of the shell, being careful not to split all the way through the lobster and crack open the shell to either side. Over a sink, wash out the organs and non-meat substances from the inner cavity, leaving the tail intact. Place the arm meat and claw meat into the cavity and set aside.

In a small mixing bowl, place the backfin crabmeat and Imperial Sauce and gently toss until thoroughly combined. Open the lobster cavities slightly and evenly distribute the crabmeat imperial between the lobsters, piling a little on top of the shell for display. Drizzle a little olive oil, Montreal seasoning and breadcrumbs on top of the crabmeat imperial and bake in a preheated 375-degree oven for about 20 minutes until the internal temperature is hot.

In a small sauté pan, place the dill, white wine, shallots and vinegar and cook until the liquids are absorbed into the dill. Cool and mix with the Hollandaise Sauce and ladle over the baked crabmeat imperial.

TOOLS

· · · · · · · · · · · ·

Measuring spoons and cup, cutting board, chef's knife, large stock pot, tongs, two mixing bowls, rubber spatula, whisk, sauté pan and ladle.

Pan-Fried Soft-Shell Crabs served with
Crusty French Bread, Thick-Cut Tomato
and Toasted Almond Butter
see recipe on
page 112

**Baked Crabmeat Imperial
between Puff Pastry with Thinly-Sliced
Country Ham and Hollandise Sauce**
see recipe on
page 116

Pecan-Crusted Flounder Fillet served over Orange-Triple Sec Demi-Glace with "Nutty" Rice, topped with a Key West Lime, Pineapple and Melon Relish

. . . .

YIELD: 6 SERVINGS

INGREDIENTS:

2 cups crushed saltine crackers
   (about 2 sleeves)

1 cup pecan pieces

2 whole eggs

1 cup whole milk

6 (6-ounce) boneless, skinless flounder fillets

1 whole pineapple, finely diced

1 whole cantaloupe, finely diced

6 tablespoons key lime juice (Joe and Nellie's)

Pinch of salt

1 tablespoon Caribbean jerk seasoning

1½ cups Demi-Glace (see page 188)

½ cup fresh-squeezed orange juice, strained

6 tablespoons Triple Sec or other orange-
   flavored liquor

½ cup blended olive oil

6 servings Seasoned "Nutty" Rice
   (see page 179)

PROCEDURE:

In a food processor, place the crushed saltines and pecan pieces and grind into a fine breading. In a mixing bowl, place the eggs and milk. Whisk until thoroughly combined. This is an egg wash. Next, take the flounder fillets and dip into the egg wash and then into the ground pecan-saltine breading. Gently press the pecan breading into the fillets, place on a wax paper-lined platter and refrigerate.

In a second mixing bowl, place the diced pineapple, cantaloupe, Key lime juice, salt and jerk seasoning. Toss the fruits with the juice and seasoning and refrigerate until time of service.

TOOLS

. . . .

Measuring spoons and cup, cutting board, chef's knife, food processor, two mixing bowls, large spoon, rubber spatula, ladle, whisk, large sauté pan and saucepan.

In a saucepan, place the Demi-Glace, orange juice and Triple Sec and cook slowly over a low heat until hot. In a large sauté pan over medium-high, heat the blended olive oil. When the oil is hot, place the breaded flounder fillets into the oil and cook on each side about

Pecan-Crusted Flounder Fillet continued

2 minutes until golden brown. Remove the flounder from the sauté pan and place on a paper-lined platter to absorb any excess oil.

It is now time to "Plate-Up." At the top of the plate, place a generous amount of the "Nutty" Rice. Then take about two or three ounces of the Triple-Sec Demi-Glace and ladle at the bottom of the plate. Take the cooked flounder fillet and lean the fish against the rice and over the sauce. To finish, spoon the Key-West relish over the fish and serve.

Fresh Flounder Fillet rolled
with Crabmeat Imperial and Thinly-Sliced
Prosciutto Ham, served with Béarnaise Sauce
and Grilled Summer Vegetables
see recipe on
page 80

Seared Salmon Fillet served over
Creamy Goat Cheese Crouton and Baby French
Green Beans, topped with Sautéed Tomatoes
and Prosciutto Ham in Caramelized Onion,
Shiitake Mushroom and Garlic Butter
see recipe on page 104

Potato-Crusted Salmon Fillet with Horseradish Cream Sauce, Sautéed Applewood Bacon, Tomatoes and Green Onions

. . . .

YIELD: 4 SERVINGS

INGREDIENTS:

2 whole extra large eggs

1 cup half-and-half cream

¼ pound saltine crackers
  (1 sleeve of the elf's brand)

8 ounces potato chips

2 tablespoons flour

4 (6-ounce) boneless, skinless salmon fillets
  (see HINT)

Nonstick cooking spray

½ pound bacon, finely-diced
  (Applewood brand or your favorite)

1 cup finely diced fresh Roma tomatoes

½ cup finely diced fresh green or spring onions

1 cup Horseradish Cream Sauce (see page 191)

> ### HINTS
> . . . .
> *Please ask your fish butcher for salmon fillets, not steaks. Remember to double-check the fillets for bones when you get home before breading.*

PROCEDURE:

In a small mixing bowl, place the eggs and cream and whip until thoroughly combined. This is called an egg wash. In a food processor, place the saltine crackers and potato chips and grind until fine. Add the flour to the mixture to complete the potato breading. Remove the breading from the processor and place in another mixing bowl. Now the breading stations are complete.

To bread the salmon, place the fillets in the egg wash for a couple of minutes to soak. Then take the fillets and place into the potato breading and coat thoroughly on both sides. When ready to cook the salmon fillets, place on a sprayed baking pan and into a preheated 375-degree oven for 10 to 14 minutes. The cooking time will depend upon the thickness of the fillets.

In a sauté pan, place the finely-diced bacon over a medium heat and cook until the bacon has rendered out all of its fat and is crispy. Lower the heat and add the diced tomato and green onions.

> ### TOOLS
> . . . .
> *Two small mixing bowls, wire whisk, baking pan or cookie pan, measuring cups and spoons, sauté pan, cutting board, chef's knife, metal spatula, food processor and ladle.*

Toss with the bacon until thoroughly combined. Turn the heat off of the bacon mixture and turn your attention to the salmon fillets.

Now, it is time to "Plate Up." Place about two ounces of the Horseradish Cream Sauce at the bottom of the plate. Next, carefully place the crusted salmon fillet on top of the sauce and top the fish with the sautéed bacon, tomatoes and green onions. Serve with some of your favorite side dishes. A couple of suggestions would be a spicy and sweet green cabbage slaw or a sour cream dressing.

Cajun Red Beans and Rice with Fresh Sea Scallops, Shrimp, Littleneck Clams, Smoked Surry Sausage and Confit Duck Leg

· ·

YIELD: 6 SERVINGS

INGREDIENTS:

6 duck legs, thigh and leg connected
¾ cup solid vegetable shortening (Crisco)
Pinch of salt and pepper
Pinch of sugar
¾ cup white rice
1 cup chicken stock
½ cup water
24 littleneck clams, washed
½ cup clam stock or water
24 sea scallops, 20 count, tag removed

24 shrimp, 16 count, shell and tail removed, butterflied and cleaned
6 (2-ounce) smoked Surry sausage, split lengthwise
1 quart Red Beans Sauce (see page 199)
12 whole crawfish, cooked and warmed
¼ cup finely diced spring onions, white part only
½ cup finely diced yellow and green bell pepper

PROCEDURE:

Let's Confit! Place the duck legs in the bottom of a shallow baking pan and spread the solid shortening over the legs. Sprinkle the duck legs with salt, pepper and sugar and place in a preheated 225-degree oven for about 2 hours (yes, 2 hours, and it does make the house smell great). When the duck legs are ready, carefully remove from the hot oil and place on a paper towel-lined platter at room temperature. This can be done ahead of time and refrigerated until needed.

Next, place the white rice, chicken stock and water in a two-quart casserole dish and into a preheated 350-degree oven for about 25 minutes. Remove the rice from the oven and stir to make sure the rice is cooked and has absorbed all of the stock. Cover and set aside. The cooked duck legs can be reheated when the rice is ready.

It is time to start the final stage. Place the littleneck clams and clam stock into a large sauté pan or wok over a medium-high heat and

TOOLS

· · · · · · · · · · · ·

Measuring spoons and cup, cutting board, chef's knife, large shallow baking pan, two-quart casserole dish, wire whisk, wooden spoon, large sauté pan or wok, tongs and six-ounce ladle.

bring to a boil. As the clams begin to open, add the sea scallops, shrimp and smoked sausage. Reduce the heat to medium, add the Red Bean Sauce and gently stir until everything is coated with the sauce. Bring the clams back to the top of the sauce so they can finish opening and add the cooked whole crawfish. Turn the heat off and cover. This will finish the cooking process as well as keep everything hot.

Now it is time to "Plate Up." In six very large bowls, place a generous amount of the cooked rice and ladle the red bean sauce and seafood into the bowls. Try to evenly distribute the seafood and sausage between the bowls and then place the confit duck leg on top. For garnish, use the warm cooked crawfish, diced spring onions and sweet bell peppers.

Fresh Virginia Rockfish
served with Sweet Cream, Flash-Fried Oysters, Local Tomatoes and Green Onions

. . . .

YIELD: 4 SERVINGS

INGREDIENTS:

4 (6- to 7-ounce) boneless, skinless fresh rockfish fillets

2 tablespoons blended olive oil

1 tablespoon Montreal seasoning, divided

1 cup solid vegetable shortening (Crisco)

16 freshly shucked oysters, the largest are called "counts"

2 whole eggs, beaten

1 cup milk

1½ cups fine ground cracker meal

Salt and pepper

1½ cups Sweet Cream and Fresh Herb Sauce (see page 204)

½ cup diced fresh tomatoes

2 tablespoons finely diced spring onions

PROCEDURE:

Take the rockfish fillets and rub them with olive oil. Sprinkle both sides of the fish fillets with about half of the Montreal seasoning. In a preheated 350-degree oven, place the rockfish fillets on a baking sheet lined with foil. Cook for about 12 minutes, depending on the thickness of the fillet. When the fillet becomes completely white through the sides, it is ready. Please do not overcook this wonderful fish.

In a separate, raised-side skillet, place the solid vegetable shortening on a medium heat until melted and hot.

Before the shortening is melted and getting hot, take the shucked oysters and place in a bowl with the beaten eggs, milk and the rest of the Montreal seasoning. Let soak for a few minutes then roll the oysters in a raised-edge pan containing the cracker meal. The breading of oysters is a careful process. I tell people I judge the quality of a seafood restaurant on a few basic items, the breading of an oyster being one. The double bread of an oyster, meaning no flour, then egg wash, then heavy breading is sinful. An oyster should only be soaked in a

> ### TOOLS
>
> . . . .
>
> *Measuring spoons and cup, cutting board and chef's knife, a baking dish, a raised-side skillet, metal turner, ladle and mixing bowl.*

seasoned egg wash then individually handled through the cracker meal, lightly patting the "yolk" or the raised center of the oyster before carefully placing on a piece of wax paper and refrigerated. The oyster should be allowed to sit uncovered in a refrigerator for at least 20 minutes before frying so the crust does not come off. Another helpful hint with oysters is to never cover them in a refrigerator, even overnight; they will become soggy and dark when frying.

I guess I have made it clear how much respect I have for the beloved "Flash-Fried Oyster." When the shortening is very hot, not smoking, but hot to a crackle of water sprinkled in the pan, place the breaded oyster by hand in the hot oil as quickly as possible. As they begin to brown, turn the oysters over to crisp both sides. When the oysters are finished frying, place on a paper-lined plate and sprinkle with salt and ground black pepper.

Now it is time to "Plate Up." First on the dinner plate, place about two to three ounces of Sweet Cream and Herb Sauce. Next, take the baked piece of fresh rockfish fillet and place over the sweet cream. Arrange four fried oysters around the rockfish fillet and top with the fresh tomato and spring onion. A suitable accompaniment for this dish may be a variety of grilled vegetables; asparagus comes to mind first and I would not serve a starch with this dish.

Rosemary-Skewered Sea Scallops served over Puff Pastry with Pernod Cream Sauce, Warm Leeks, Tomatoes and Shiitake Mushrooms, and served with Grilled Asparagus

. . . .

YIELD: 6 SERVINGS, 2 SKEWERS PER SERVING

INGREDIENTS:

3 pounds fresh sea scallops, 20 count, tags removed

½ cup blended olive oil

Salt and pepper

12 (6-inch) fresh rosemary stems

3 squares puff pastry, cut in triangles about five inches across

Nonstick cooking spray

1 whole egg

2 tablespoons water

3 tablespoons white wine

½ cup fresh leeks, white part only, cut in half then cut in half moons

2 cups sliced shiitake mushroom caps

1 pound fresh asparagus, cut, peeled and lightly blanched

1 tablespoon olive oil

1 tablespoon Montreal seasoning

1½ cups Pernod Cream Sauce (see page 194)

½ cup diced fresh Roma tomatoes

PROCEDURE:

In a large mixing bowl, place the sea scallops, blended olive oil, salt and pepper. Toss the scallops until thoroughly coated. Take most of the rosemary off the stem by pulling against the direction the leaves are growing and strip the stem about three-quarters of the way. Skewer the scallops onto the cleaned rosemary stems. Next, place the puff pastry triangles on a sprayed baking pan. Beat together the egg and water and brush over the pastry. Bake in a preheated 375-degree oven for about 10 minutes or until risen and browned. Remove from the oven and let rest. In a small saucepan, place the white wine, leeks and shiitake mushrooms. Heat until warm and until the leeks are still crisp but the mushrooms are limp. On a hot grill, place the scallop skewers and the asparagus lightly drizzled with olive oil and sprinkled with Montreal seasoning. Cook until the asparagus is tender and the scallops are firm and white. Heat the Pernod Cream Sauce and now let's "Plate-Up."

TOOLS

. . . .

Measuring spoons and cup, cutting board, chef's knife, mixing bowl rubber spatula, baking dish, two saucepans, whisk, ladle, hot grill and tongs.

Rosemary-Skewered Sea Scallops continued

In the center of the plate, take the puff pastry triangle and cut the pastry horizontally, creating two half triangles. Place the bottom triangle on the plate. Place about half of the warmed mushroom mixture on top of the pastry and about two ounces of the Pernod sauce over the mushrooms. Set two of the scallop skewers on top of the mushrooms, then the other half of the mushroom mixture, and more sauce. Drizzle the freshly diced Roma tomatoes around the pastry. Lastly, set the top half of the pastry on top like a book and lean the grilled asparagus against the finished scallop pastry dish.

Seared Salmon Fillet served over Creamy Goat Cheese Crouton and Baby French Green Beans, topped with Sautéed Tomatoes and Prosciutto Ham in Caramelized Onion, Shiitake Mushroom and Garlic Butter

. . . .

YIELD: 6 SERVINGS

INGREDIENTS:

2 tablespoons blended olive oil
¼ cup finely diced yellow onion
1 tablespoon finely diced fresh garlic
½ pound shiitake mushroom caps, sliced
1 tablespoon fresh chopped parsley
Dash of Tabasco sauce
½ pound sweet butter, softened
1 tablespoon finely diced fresh chives
¼ pound cream cheese, softened

¼ pound goat cheese, softened
6 thick-cut slices Italian bread
6 (6-ounce) boneless, skinless salmon fillets
Salt and freshly ground black pepper
Nonstick cooking spray
½ cup finely diced fresh Roma tomatoes
¼ pound Prosciutto ham, finely diced
¾ pound baby French green beans, blanched in lightly salted water

PROCEDURE:

In a sauté pan, place the blended olive oil and yellow onion and cook over a medium heat until the onions begin to caramelize and turn brown. Add the diced garlic and the shiitake mushrooms and stir until the garlic is roasted and the mushrooms begin to go limp. Remove from heat, stir in the chopped parsley and Tabasco sauce and set aside to cool. In a freestanding mixer, whip the softened butter on medium speed until smooth. Add the cooled, caramelized onion-mushroom mixture to the butter and whip at a low speed until thoroughly combined. Transfer to a bowl and refrigerate until time of service.

TOOLS

. . . .

Measuring spoons and cup, cutting board, chef's knife, three sauté pans, rubber spatula, freestanding mixer, two baking pans, metal turner, tongs and ladle.

Back in the mixer, place the chives and softened cream and goat cheeses and blend into a creamy spread. Remove from the mixer and spread the creamy goat cheese mixture onto the Italian bread. Loosely cover until time of service.

Season the salmon fillets with salt and black pepper and spray a large sauté pan with cooking spray. Place the salmon fillets in the sauté pan on a medium-high heat and sear the fillets on both sides for about 2 minutes. After searing, transfer the salmon fillets to a baking pan and into a preheated 375-degree oven for about 8 to 10 minutes, depending on the thickness of the fillets.

As the salmon fillets are finishing in the oven, the creamy croutons can be placed in the same oven for the last 2 minutes of cooking time. In a sauté pan, place the caramelized onion butter, tomatoes and Prosciutto ham over a medium heat and cook until hot. Reheat the blanched baby green beans until warm and now it is time to "Plate-Up."

First, take a creamy goat cheese crouton and place at the top-center of the plate. Next, arrange the warm baby beans to the right of the crouton at about two o'clock and set the seared salmon fillet against the crouton at the bottom center of the plate. Pour the sautéed ham, tomatoes and mushroom butter over the salmon fillet and serve.

Fresh Sea Scallop, Shrimp, Crawfish and Littleneck Clam "Étouffée" served with Sticky Rice, Smoked Sausage, Tomatoes and Green Onions

· ·

YIELD: 6 SERVINGS

INGREDIENTS: *(for the Rice)*

1 cup dry white rice

2 cups water

1 cup chicken stock

Pinch of salt and white pepper

INGREDIENTS: *(for the Sauce)*

1 cup julienne yellow onion

1 cup bias-cut celery

2 tablespoons olive oil

¼ teaspoon white pepper

¼ teaspoon ground black pepper

¼ teaspoon ground red or cayenne pepper

¼ teaspoon crushed red pepper flakes

½ teaspoon paprika

½ teaspoon dried thyme leaves

½ teaspoon dried basil leaves

½ teaspoon dried oregano leaves

3 bay leaves

1 tablespoon hand-chopped fresh garlic

1 cup diced fresh Roma tomatoes

2 cups chicken stock

3 cups beef stock

8 tablespoons butter (1 stick)

6 tablespoons flour

12 (2-ounce) smoked Surry sausage links or your favorite, halved lengthwise

36 littleneck clams, closed and washed

24 whole crawfish, washed and steamed

24 shrimp, 21 count, shell and tail removed, butterflied and cleaned

30 sea scallops, 25 count, tag removed

PROCEDURE:

In a saucepan, place the rice, water, stock, salt and pepper and stir until thoroughly incorporated. Cover, place in a 350-degree oven and cook for about 30 minutes.

TOOLS

· · · · · · · · · · · ·

Measuring spoons and cup, cutting board, chef's knife, sauté pan, two-quart saucepan, two quart casserole dish for rice, smaller sauté pan for roux, three wire whisks, wooden spoon and six-ounce ladle.

To make the sauce, take the onion, celery and olive oil and place in a sauté pan over medium heat. Cook until the celery begins to soften and add all the spices, dried herbs and garlic. Stir until a rich color and aroma occurs. Next, add the tomatoes and transfer to a larger saucepan. Add the chicken and beef stocks and bring to a simmer.

In a separate saucepan, melt the butter. Add the flour and cook over a medium heat, stirring constantly until smooth. Cook the smooth roux for a minute then remove from heat. Add the cooked roux to the simmering sauce and increase the heat to medium-high, stirring the entire time. The sauce should begin to thicken. At the first sign of a boil, reduce the heat to medium-low and add the littleneck clams and split smoked sausage links. Stir the clams into the sauce to allow them to heat and begin to open. This is a very important time to continue stirring the sauce, not only to prevent sticking, but also to rotate the clams to the surface. As the clams begin to open let them stay on top of the sauce. Now reduce the heat to low and add the whole cooked crawfish, shrimp and sea scallops. Once again, continue to stir for about 2 minutes. The shrimp and scallops will cook very quickly. Turn the heat off and stir gently so the sauce does not stick and cover loosely until time of service.

It's time to "Plate Up." In the corner of each of 6 large-rimmed bowls, put a scoop (about a cup) of the cooked sticky rice. Then, with a large ladle, scoop the sauce and seafood evenly between the 6 bowls. Garnish with some diced fresh Roma tomatoes and green onions.

Fresh Sea Scallops, Shrimp and Lobster served in a Parmesan Cheese and Dill Cream Sauce over Linguine with Littleneck Clams, Mussels, Tomatoes, Spring Onions and Crusty Garlic Bread

. . . .

YIELD: 6 SERVINGS

INGREDIENTS:

2 cups water

18 littleneck clams, closed and washed

18 mussels, washed and beards removed

1 cup white wine

1 pound shrimp, 16 to 20 count, shell removed, butterflied, deveined and cleaned

¾ pound sea scallops, 20 count, tags removed

1 quart Parmesan Cheese-Dill Cream Sauce (see page 196)

3 (1½-pound) whole Maine lobsters, cooked, tail and claw meat removed and chopped

6 large slices French bread

½ pound Garlic-Shallot Butter (see page 176)

1½ pounds cooked linguine

1 cup finely diced fresh Roma tomatoes

½ cup finely diced fresh spring onions

½ cup shaved Parmesan cheese

PROCEDURE:

In a large saucepan, place the water, littleneck clams and mussels over a medium heat and simmer until the mussels and clams begin to open. Add the white wine, shrimp and scallops. Continue cooking until the shrimp begin to turn red, the scallops white and the clams are open. Remove from heat and carefully pour off the wine and water. Do not pour into a strainer. Just pour off the liquid from the side of the pan. Now add the Parmesan Cheese Cream Sauce and the lobster meat and simmer until hot. Place the slices of French bread on a baking pan and cover with Garlic-Shallot Butter. Place in a preheated 375-degree oven for about 5 minutes until butter is melted and bread is crusty.

TOOLS

. . . .

Measuring spoons and cup, cutting board, chef's knife, large saucepan, tongs, rubber spatula, ladle, baking pan, metal turner and large spoon.

To "Plate-Up," in large pasta bowls place about four ounces of cooked linguine. Carefully remove three each of the clams and mussels and arrange them on the outer sides of the pasta bowl. Pour a majority of the sauce over the pasta centers and evenly distribute three

Fresh Sea Scallops, Shrimp and Lobster continued

shrimp, three or four scallops and half of the lobster meat into each of the pasta bowls. You don't want to get anyone mad about not getting one or the other. Pour the remaining sauce over the seafood. Sprinkle with the diced Roma tomatoes, spring onions and shaved Parmesan cheese, and serve with a slice of the crusty garlic bread.

Fresh Shad Roe served with
Crisp Bacon, Tomatoes, Grilled Sweet Onions,
Spring Onions and Poached Eggs

. . . .

YIELD: 4 SERVINGS

When our seafood purveyors call us in March and tell us they have shad roe, we know it is the first sign of spring. The first of the roe will be harvested from Georgia or South Carolina. Then as the warmer weather comes north, so will the shad, and roe harvested from North Carolina and Virginia will be available. The local shad roe is sometimes nicknamed "York River caviar."

INGREDIENTS:

12 slices thick-cut bacon
4 (6- to 8-ounce) sets fresh shad roe (see HINT)
Salt and pepper
½ cup flour
3 tablespoons butter
1 tablespoon finely chopped garlic
1 medium-size red onion, cut julienne
½ cup finely diced Roma tomatoes
1 tablespoon finely chopped shallot
1 tablespoon Montreal seasoning
1 tablespoon fresh squeezed lemon juice
2 tablespoons finely chopped parsley
1 tablespoon finely diced spring onions
1 quart water
1 teaspoon white vinegar
4 whole eggs

> ## HINT
> . . . .
> *If you are not familiar with shad roe, it is the eggs sacks of the shad fish, a Native American fish. The shad usually decide to spawn beginning in mid- to late-February until as late as early- to mid-April. Their spawning grounds are the tributary rivers off the coast of the southeastern United States. The first areas will be in Georgia and South Carolina, then up north to North Carolina and Virginia. The spawning of the shad is usually a more reliable sign of the actual arrival of spring to the southeastern region of the United States than a groundhog with television cameras in Pennsylvania.*
> *Be careful of the Jack fish roe sometimes being passed off as shad roe. In our area of Virginia, we look forward to the first signs of "York River caviar."*

PROCEDURE:

In a large sauté pan, cook the thick-cut bacon over medium heat until crispy. Remove the bacon from the pan and turn the heat off but leave bacon fat in pan until ready to cook the shad roe. Lay the sets of shad roe out on a plate and lightly salt and pepper both sides. Dust the shad roe with flour. Turn back on the heat under the sauté pan containing the bacon fat. When the fat gets hot, place the floured shad roe in the pan and reduce the heat to medium. Cook for approximately 4 minutes on each side or until the shad roe begins to change into a lighter colored set of firm eggs. Remove from the pan and once again turn the heat off under the sauté pan. If the bacon grease can take one more minute of cooking try to use it. If it is smoking and burnt, discard the bacon fat and use the three tablespoons of butter. In the butter or fat, add the chopped garlic, red onions, tomatoes, shallots and Montreal seasoning. Sauté until golden. Add the fresh lemon juice and parsley and remove from heat.

In a separate saucepan, place the water and white vinegar and bring to a boil. Reduce the heat to medium-high and add the whole eggs, cracking one at a time into the water, stirring in a clockwise fashion very slowly. The object is to keep the eggs separated, not to make scrambled eggs. The vinegar's purpose is to draw the yolk back into the center, thus forming a poached egg. When the egg is soft poached, carefully remove with a slotted spoon and place on a paper towel-covered plate.

It is now time "To Plate Up." First on your plate, place the cooked shad roe in the center. Top with three slices of the cooked thick-cut bacon. Pour the sautéed garlic-shallot mixture over the top. The center piece of the dish is the poached egg. A great garnish for this dish would be toast points, depending on mealtime. If a brunch, cheese grits; if dinner, maybe some grilled vegetables.

TOOLS

· · · · · · · · · · · · ·

Measuring spoons and cup, cutting board, chef's knife, large sauté pan, metal spatula, four-quart saucepan and slotted spoon.

Pan-Fried Soft-Shell Crabs served with Crusty French Bread, Thick-Cut Tomato and Toasted Almond Butter

. . . .

YIELD: 4 SERVINGS OF 3 EACH

The next local favorite to emerge in the late spring is soft-shell crabs. If conditions are favorable in late April or early May, during the full moon, the local crab shedders will work through the night. Although the season seems to be shorter each year, the demand and interest for the soft-shell crab never seems to diminish.

INGREDIENTS:

12 fresh soft-shell crabs, primes
¾ cup blended olive oil, divided
Salt and pepper
2 cups flour
8 tablespoons sweet butter (1 stick)
1 small sweet red bell pepper, finely diced

¼ cup sliced blanched almonds
2 tablespoons finely chopped fresh parsley
Juice of 1 lemon
8 (1-inch thick) slices French bread, toasted
8 thick slices fresh tomato

PROCEDURE:

To clean the crabs, use a pair of scissors to remove the face. Reach under the side shell and remove the lungs and under the crab, the apron, which looks like a flap. Gently squeeze the loose insides from the crab through the front.

In a large sauté pan over medium heat, place ½ cup of the olive oil. Season the cleaned soft-shell crabs with salt and pepper and dredge in the flour. When thoroughly coated with the flour, place in the hot olive oil, shell side down. Cook for approximately 2 minutes on this side then turn over and do the same on the bottom side of the crab, until both sides are cooked and crispy. Turn the heat off from the sauté pan and remove the crabs to a landing plate covered with a paper towel to catch any of the excess oil. Pour the unwanted oil from the sauté pan and use this same pan to make the toasted almond butter. Place the butter in the pan with the diced red bell peppers. When peppers are

> ### TOOLS
> . . . .
> *Measuring spoons and cup, cutting board, chef's knife, sauté pan, metal spatula and ladle.*

softened, add the almonds and a pinch of salt and stir until the almonds begin to toast. Add the parsley and lemon juice and turn off the heat and stir.

Time to "Plate up." First, take one soft-shell crab and lean a piece of the French bread next to it, then a slice of tomato, then a crab again, repeating until the third crab is at end of the half-circle. Pour the toasted almond butter over the entire half-circle of crab, bread and tomato. A great accompaniment for this dish is some grilled spring asparagus.

What To Look For and How To Clean Soft-Shelled Crabs

The blue crab will look to molt or lose its existing shell in the spring along the Mid-Atlantic regional waters. During this time the crabs would look for sanctuary in the tributaries off the major rivers in order to achieve this new coat of honor and not leave themselves vulnerable to attack. The "natural time" of this experience is usually during the first full moon in May and will at times last through July. There are "unnatural time" tanks set up to fool the crabs in order for this process to take place all Spring long.

First and foremost only buy live soft shell crabs, pass on any that are lifeless or dead. Remember you eat the entire crab when it is soft shelled. The claws are soft so do not be afraid of this crab. To clean a soft shell blue crab be quick and painless as possible, holding the crab by the back area take a sharp pair of scissors and clip off the entire face region. Next pull up on each side of the top shell of the crab and remove the gills of the crab, it will be the top spongy area beneath the shell. Now turn the crab over and pull off the mantle, a lower flap on the crab. As a side not to distinguish a male blue crab from a female, considering where we live it is said, "The male mantle or flap looks like the Washington Monument and the females resembles the Capital Dome." After pulling off the bottom flap then face the crab down and squeeze the guts, organs, natural tartar sauce or whatever you want to call out of the cavity before starting your recipe.

Sautéed Gulf Shrimp and Lump Crabmeat served over Angel Hair Pasta with Sun-Dried Tomato Sauce, Parmesan Cheese, Spring Onions and Crusty Garlic Bread

. . . .

YIELD: 6 SERVINGS

INGREDIENTS:

8 tablespoons butter (1 stick), softened

1 tablespoon chopped fresh garlic

1 tablespoon finely chopped fresh parsley

Juice of 1 lemon

2 dashes of Tabasco sauce

Pinch of ground black pepper

12 slices thick-cut French bread

3 cups Creamy Sun-Dried Tomato Sauce (see page 203)

2 tablespoons olive oil

2 dozen shrimp, 16 count, shell and tail removed, butterflied and cleaned

½ cup finely diced spring onions, white part only

3 cups cooked angel hair pasta, oiled and room temperature

1 pound fresh jumbo lump crabmeat, shell removed

½ cup finely grated aged Parmesan cheese

PROCEDURE:

In a food processor, place the softened butter, garlic, parsley, lemon juice, Tabasco sauce and pepper. Blend until smooth and creamy. Spread the garlic butter on the thick-cut French bread and set aside until ready to serve. In a double boiler setup, place the previously finished Sun-Dried Tomato Sauce and reheat slowly. In a large sauté pan, heat the olive oil over a medium heat until hot, then add the shrimp and cook until the shrimp begin to curl and turn white. Please do not over-cook the shrimp. Add the spring onion and cooked angel hair pasta and gently toss until thoroughly mixed. Reduce the heat to low and add the lump crabmeat and once again toss gently to incorporate the crabmeat. Turn off the heat. Place the garlic bread in a preheated 350-degree oven for about six minutes.

To "Plate Up," place the pasta and seafood mixture with a pair of tongs in a large pile in the center of the plates. Pour about four ounces of the Sun-Dried Tomato Sauce over the pasta. Arrange the shrimp and lump crabmeat evenly on the top of the sauce. Lastly, sprinkle the Parmesan cheese on top and serve with two slices of the garlic bread.

TOOLS

. . . .

Measuring spoons and cup, cutting board, chef's knife, food processor, rubber spatula, baking pan, double boiler setup, large sauté pan and tongs.

Grilled Yellowfin Tuna Steak
served Medium-Rare over "Berret's" Steak Sauce, topped with Flash-Fried Onion Straw, Tomatoes and Tarragon Radish Sour Cream

. . . .

YIELD: 6 SERVINGS

INGREDIENTS:

6 (7-ounce, 1-inch thick) fresh yellowfin tuna steaks

2 tablespoons olive oil

2 tablespoons Montreal seasoning

1 large yellow onion, very thinly sliced

2 cups flour

2 tablespoons cornstarch

1 quart solid vegetable shortening (Crisco)

¾ cup Berret's Steak Sauce (see page 202)

1 cup finely diced fresh Roma tomatoes

½ cup Tarragon-Radish Sour Cream Dressing (see page 71)

PROCEDURE:

On a large plate, place the tuna steaks and drizzle with the olive oil. Sprinkle with the Montreal seasoning and rub the steaks until thoroughly covered. On a hot grill, place the steaks and grill each side about 2 to 3 minutes, depending on the intensity of the heat, until the steaks are about medium-rare. If your preference is that the steaks be cooked more, go ahead and cook longer but try not to dry the tuna out. In a small mixing bowl, toss the thinly sliced onions with the flour and the cornstarch until thoroughly coated. In a large pot half-full of hot vegetable oil, submerge the flour-coated onions and cook until crispy (only a couple of minutes at most). Remove from the hot oil and place on a paper towel-lined plate.

It is now time to "Plate-Up." Ladle two ounces of Berret's Steak Sauce onto the bottom of the plate and place the cooked tuna steak on top of the sauce. Pile a generous amount of the fried onion straw on top of the steak and sprinkle with the diced fresh tomatoes. Just before service, drizzle the Tarragon-Radish Sour Cream Dressing on top of the tuna steak and serve. The recommended accompaniments to the tuna steak would be creamed Anna potatoes and some grilled vegetables, like asparagus or summer squashes.

TOOLS

. . . .

Measuring spoons and cup, cutting board, chef's knife, large plate, hot grill, small mixing bowl, large pot for frying, strainer to remove fried foods and ladle.

Baked Crabmeat Imperial between Puff Pastry with Thinly-Sliced Country Ham and Hollandaise Sauce

. . . .

YIELD: 6 SERVINGS

This Virginia combination has been on menus at the restaurants that I have worked at for over twenty years. The presentation has changed over the years but never the ingredients.

INGREDIENTS:

3 (5-inch) squares puff pastry (see HINT)

1 whole egg

2 tablespoons water

1½ pounds jumbo lump crabmeat, picked and shell removed

1 cup Imperial Sauce (see page 192)

Nonstick cooking spray

6 ounces Virginia country ham, thinly sliced

¾ cup Hollandaise Sauce (see page 190)

HINT

. . . .

Make your own puff pastry if you like, otherwise there are frozen pastry sheets or squares that are very fine.

PROCEDURE:

To start, take the frozen puff pastry squares or sheets and cut each into two triangle while semi-frozen. It is much easier to cut the pastry while just out of the freezer a couple of minutes. Set the cut triangles on a lightly greased baking pan and let sit until completely thawed, just a couple of minutes. It is not necessary to brush the top of the pastry with half water, half egg mixture but it does give it a nice golden sheen when baked. Cook the pastry as shown on packaging instructions, usually about ten minutes in a preheated 375-degree oven. When done, set aside until time of service.

In a small mixing bowl, toss the crabmeat and Imperial Sauce and gently combine until crabmeat is thoroughly coated. On a lightly sprayed or parchment-covered baking dish, make six even portions of the crabmeat mixture and place in a preheated 375-degree oven to bake for about 12 minutes. Remove from oven and it's time to "Plate-Up."

TOOLS

. . . .

Measuring spoons and cup, cutting board, chef's knife, two baking dishes, two mixing bowls, rubber spatula, whisk, pastry brush and ladle.

Baked Crabmeat Imperial continued

For assembly, take the cooked but room temperature pastry triangles and cut in half horizontally (that always confuses me), like a hamburger bun with a top and a bottom triangle. Place the bottom triangle on the plate, the thinly sliced country ham on top of the bottom pastry and the baked crabmeat imperial on the top of the ham. Ladle about two ounces of Hollandaise Sauce over the crabmeat imperial and place the top half of the pastry on the very top.

Add a seasonal accompaniment of grilled asparagus, warm spinach, fresh tomatoes or your favorites.

SEAFOOD BAKED IN PARCHMENT

SEAFOOD BAKED IN PARCHMENT

. . . .

Cajun-Spiced Fresh Grouper and
Gulf Shrimp Baked in Parchment Paper, 122

Fresh Dolphin Fish, Sea Scallops and
Escargot Baked in Parchment Paper, 124

Fresh Flounder and Sea Scallops
Baked in Parchment Paper, 126

Fresh Sea Scallops and Lobster Meat
Baked in Parchment Paper, 128

Fresh Shrimp, Mussels and Lobster Meat
Baked in Parchment Paper, 132

Fresh Monkfish, Sea Scallops and Mussels
Baked in Parchment Paper, 136

Fresh Pompano, Lump Crabmeat and Mussels
Baked in Parchment Paper, 140

Sesame-Crusted Salmon Fillet
and Shrimp Baked in Parchment Paper, 144

Fresh Sea Scallops and Shrimp Baked in Parchment Paper, 146

Fresh Red Snapper Fillet, Littleneck Clams
and Calamari Baked in Parchment Paper,   148

PAPERBACK WRITER

· · · · · · · · · · ·

When I first thought about writing a cookbook, I thought of all the "Seafood Baked in Parchments" that we feature on our daily specials at Berret's and River's Inn Brunch menu. The first title thought that come to mind for a book like this was 'Paperback Writer.' I love the name for this chapter because of the song, the Beatles and the times.

Day in and day out, the number one selling dinner entrée sold at Berret's is the "Seafood Baked in Parchment."

The history of seafood baked in parchment has a couple of twists and turns. The most reliable is the chef who wanted to impress his special guests. They were famous balloonists and he wanted his dish to resemble a balloon. In essence, the cooking of food in parchment is similar to cooking items sealed in aluminum foil over an open grill at the family barbecue. The object is to seal all the juices, aroma and flavor until the dish is placed in front of the guest.

There are two very important things to remember in assembling parchments. The number one thing is the type of fold you will take to accomplish the goal, which is to seal the foods in. Secondly the assemble of "the mise en place." This cooking term simply means the gathering of all ingredients before preparation begins.

A parchment is viewed as a complete meal; it must be able to stand on its own. A theme needs to be established – an example would be seafood with pasta and garlic butter, like scampi. The theme is very fun and leads to some unusual ideas. Remember the assembly will include raw foods, partially cooked foods, and fully cooked foods.

The simple steaming of foods in their own juices and flavors creates a natural aromatic combination. Cooking seafood in parchment can also be a very healthy cooking method depending on the contents chosen, although most of the recipes you will see in this chapter include a "compound" butter blended with either fresh herbs or other ingredients that may not make the top-ten non-calorie list. Simply leave out the butter or other ingredients you may not want. Make your own parchment combinations, remembering that is part of the fun of cooking.

Cajun-Spiced Fresh Grouper and Gulf Shrimp Baked in Parchment Paper with Collard Greens, "Dirty Rice", Tomatoes, Sweet Bell Peppers and Tasso Ham Crawfish Butter

. . . .

YIELD: 6 SERVINGS

INGREDIENTS:

3 pieces bacon, diced

1 small yellow onion, finely diced

2 pounds fresh collard greens, washed

½ cup water

¼ cup apple cider vinegar

2 tablespoons cracked black pepper

¾ pound sweet butter (3 sticks), softened

½ pound cooked crawfish tail meat, finely chopped

¼ cup Tasso ham or Cajun spiced ham, finely diced

Nonstick cooking spray

1½ cups Berret's "Dirty Rice" (see page 175)

6 (4- to 5-ounce) boneless, skinless fresh grouper fillets

2 tablespoons blackening seasoning

1 pound shrimp, 16 to 20 count, shell removed, butterflied cleaned

1 cup red and yellow bell peppers, cut into thin strips

½ cup finely diced fresh Roma tomatoes

PROCEDURE:

In a large saucepan over medium heat place the diced bacon and cook until the meat is crispy and all the fat has been rendered. Add the onion and cook until translucent. Next, add the collard greens, water, vinegar and cracked black pepper and cook until the greens are wilted down to a soft consistency. Remove the collards from the pan, drain and set aside.

In a freestanding mixer, blend the sweet butter until smooth. Add the cooked crawfish tail meat and Tasso ham to the butter. Blend on a medium speed until the crawfish-ham butter is once again smooth. Use a rubber spatula to scrape down the sides of the mixing bowl to fully incorporate all of the crawfish and ham into the butter. With the butter ready, it is time to assemble the parchment. First, spray the cooking spray on the inside surface of the

TOOLS

. . . .

Measuring spoons and cup, cutting board, chef's knife, small mixing bowl, rubber spatula, baking pan, freestanding mixer and large spoon or scoop.

parchment paper before assembly. This will reduce the chance of the food sticking to the paper after cooking.

When assembling a parchment, remember to start the food in the middle of one-half of the entire paper. The other half needs to come over the top and begin the fold.

The order of the assembly is:

A bed of cooked, drained collard greens

Next a scoop of "Dirty Rice"

The grouper fillet sprinkled with the blackening seasoning

Three shrimp

The thin cut bell peppers

The diced Roma tomatoes

A "healthy" scoop of the crawfish-Tasso ham butter

Place in a preheated 375-degree oven for about 35 minutes; remove from oven and serve. A side dish of sour cream, fresh spring onions and some ice-cold tea or beer would be a great accompaniment.

Fresh Dolphin Fish, Sea Scallops and Escargot Baked in Parchment Paper with Arugula, Tortellini Pasta, Roma Tomatoes, Stuffed Queen Olives, Grilled Sweet Onions, Goat Cheese and Pommery Mustard-Surry Bacon Vinaigrette Dressing

YIELD: 6 SERVINGS

INGREDIENTS:

1 sweet red onion, cut into ¼-inch julienne pieces

1 tablespoon blended olive oil

Salt and ground black pepper

½ pound halved fresh Roma tomatoes

¼ cup halved stuffed queen olives

½ pound goat cheese, crumbled

¾ cup Pommery Mustard and Surry Bacon Vinaigrette Dressing (see page 55)

Nonstick cooking spray

½ pound fresh arugula, stems removed

1 pound tortellini pasta, cooked, cooled and lightly oiled

2 pounds dolphin fish fillet, skin removed and cut into strips

1½ pounds sea scallops, 20 count, tags removed

18 escargot, out of the shell

PROCEDURE:

In a small raised grill sauté pan place the julienne cut red onions with the tablespoon of olive oil and sprinkle with salt and black pepper. Cook until the onions begin to brown, then remove from the pan and set aside. In a small mixing bowl toss the cut Roma tomatoes, queen olives, goat cheese and grilled onions until thoroughly combined. Next, warm the mustard-bacon vinaigrette dressing to just above room temperature before assembling the parchments. Now it is time to assemble the parchments. Spray the parchment paper with the cooking spray before assembly.

TOOLS

Measuring spoons and cup, cutting board, chef's knife, small mixing bowl, rubber spatula, baking pan, grill or sauté pan and ladle.

The order of the assembly is:

    A bed of fresh arugula leaves

    Next the cooked tortellini pasta

    The dolphin fish strips, spread out

    Five to six scallops

    Three escargots

    The tomato, olive, onion and cheese mixture

    A two-ounce ladle of the mustard-bacon dressing

Place the parchments in a preheated 375-degree oven and bake for about 30 minutes. Remove from the oven and serve. A good side dish would be virgin olive oil or aïoli, and some warm Italian bread or flat bread.

Fresh Flounder and Sea Scallops Baked in Parchment Paper with Linguine, Sun-Dried Tomatoes, Basil, Pine Nuts, Parmesan Cheese and Garlic-Shallot Butter

. . . .

YIELD: 4 SERVINGS

INGREDIENTS:

6 ounces butter (1½ sticks), softened

1 tablespoon pureed fresh garlic

1 tablespoon pureed fresh shallots

2 tablespoons finely chopped fresh parsley

1 teaspoon Worcestershire sauce

½ teaspoon ground black pepper

Pinch of sea salt or table salt

3 tablespoons sun-dried tomatoes

2 tablespoons water

Nonstick cooking spray

½ pound linguine, cooked, cooled and oiled

1 pound boneless, skinless fresh flounder fillet, cut into about 2-ounce portions

¾ pound fresh sea scallops, 20 to 30 count, tags removed

3 tablespoons fresh basil leaves, cut gently into strips

¼ cup grated aged Parmesan cheese

2 tablespoons pine nuts

PROCEDURE:

The first item to make is the garlic-shallot butter; place the softened butter in a food processor and blend on a medium-low speed until smooth. When smooth add the pureed garlic, shallots, chopped parsley, Worcestershire sauce, black pepper and sea salt. Blend at medium speed until thoroughly combined. Remove from the processor and refrigerate until needed. This butter has many names; scampi, escargot, Maitre De Hotel or house butter are examples.

Next are the sun-dried tomatoes. Place the tomatoes in a small bowl and cover with the water. Let the tomatoes rest for a few minutes as they soften and come back to life. When soft, strain the water off and rinse the tomatoes with fresh water to remove any residual salt. Place the rinsed tomatoes on a paper towel. The paper towel will absorb any excess water. Cut the tomatoes into julienne strips and set aside. Spray the parchment paper with cooking spray

> ### TOOLS
> . . . .
> *Measuring spoons and cup, cutting board, chef's knife, food processor small mixing bowl, parchment paper and cookie tray.*

before assembly. As noted in the "Paperback-Writer" prologue, having all of "mise en place" together before assembly is a must.

The order of assembly is:

A bed of cooked linguine

The flounder fillet, spread out

The sea scallops, spread out

The fresh basil

The sun-dried tomatoes

The Parmesan cheese

The pine nuts

A good two-ounces of the garlic-shallot butter

Place in a preheated 375-degree oven and bake for 30 minutes. Remove from the oven and serve.

Some side dish suggestions would be additional Parmesan cheese and some toasted garlic French bread.

Fresh Sea Scallops and Lobster Meat Baked in Parchment Paper with Kale, Roasted Red Bliss Potatoes, Carrots, Mini Corn on the Cob, Roma Tomatoes and Lemon-Pepper Butter

. . . .

YIELD: 6 SERVINGS

INGREDIENTS:

1 pound red bliss potatoes, cut into quarters

2 tablespoons olive oil

Salt and pepper to taste

¾ pound butter (3 sticks)

Zest and juice of 3 lemons

1 teaspoon salt

1 tablespoon cracked black pepper

Nonstick cooking spray

½ pound fresh kale, stems removed and washed thoroughly

1½ pounds lobster meat, removed from shell, cut into pieces

1½ pounds sea scallops, 20 count, tags removed

1 cup fresh carrots, cut into thin strips

3 ears corn on the cob, blanched in water and halved crosswise

6 Roma tomatoes, cut into quarters

PROCEDURE:

In a small mixing bowl place the cut red bliss potatoes, olive oil and salt and black pepper to taste; toss the potatoes until thoroughly coated. Place the potatoes on a baking pan and into a preheated 250-degree oven. Bake for about 45 minutes. Remove the potatoes from the oven and set aside to cool at room temperature. In a freestanding or hand mixer, blend the butter until smooth. Then add the lemon zest, juice, 1 teaspoon salt and 1 tablespoon cracked black pepper into the smooth butter and blend on a medium speed until once again smooth. Use a rubber spatula to get all the pepper and lemon zest from the sides of the mixing bowl and into the butter. When the butter is ready, it is time to assemble the parchments. Spray the piece of parchment paper with the cooking spray before assembly.

TOOLS

. . . .

Measuring spoons and cup, cutting board, chef's knife, small mixing bowl, rubber spatula, baking pan, freestanding mixer and large spoon or scoop.

The order of the assembly is:

A bed of fresh kale

The cooked red bliss potatoes

The lobster meat, evenly distributed to the six parchments

Five to six scallops

The matchstick carrots

The mini corn on the cob

The quartered Roma tomatoes

A "healthy" scoop of the lemon-pepper butter

Place into a preheated 375-degree oven and bake for about 30 minutes. Remove from oven and serve, usually with some Old Bay seasoning, more fresh lemon halves, melted butter and some crusty French bread.

This view shows the initial construction to the original Coleman Bridge as well as the existing "ferry-car" service between Yorktown and Gloucester Point.

Gloucester Point in the 1930's as viewed looking down the dirt road leading down to where The Virginia Institute of Marine Science currently resides.

This view of the magnificent original Coleman Bridge from the shoreline.

Fresh Shrimp, Mussels and Lobster Meat Baked in Parchment Paper with Lemon Couscous, Spinach, Grilled Sweet Peppers and Onions, Roma Tomatoes and Feta Cheese-Chive Butter

. . . .

YIELD: 6 SERVINGS

INGREDIENTS:

1 cup chicken stock

½ cup dry couscous

Zest and juice of 6 lemons

2 tablespoons Montreal seasoning, divided

¼ cup olive oil, divided

1 cup red and yellow sweet bell peppers, cut into thin strips

½ cup sweet red onions, cut into thin strips

½ pound butter (2 sticks), softened

¼ pound feta cheese

1 tablespoon finely chopped garlic

1 teaspoon cracked black pepper

2 tablespoons finely diced fresh chives

Nonstick cooking spray

½ pound fresh spinach leaves, stems removed

2 pounds shrimp, 16 to 20 count, shell removed, butterflied and cleaned

3 (1½-pound) whole Maine lobsters, steamed, tail and claw meat removed and chopped

18 mussels in the shell, cleaned and beards removed

½ pound fresh Roma tomatoes, cut in halves

PROCEDURE:

In a saucepan bring the chicken stock to a boil. In a casserole dish, add the dry couscous and pour the boiling chicken stock over it. Stir the couscous and stock until thoroughly combined and then cover. Let sit covered for about 30 minutes until the couscous has absorbed all the liquid. Remove the cover and stir in the lemon zest, lemon juice, 1 tablespoon of the Montreal seasoning and 2 tablespoons of the olive oil. Set aside and stir occasionally until cool.

> ### TOOLS
> . . . .
> *Measuring spoons and cup, cutting board, chefs knife, small mixing bowl, rubber spatula, baking pan, raised-grill sauté pan, freestanding mixer and a large spoon or scoop.*

In a small mixing bowl place the thin sliced sweet bell peppers, onions, one tablespoon of Montreal seasoning and two tablespoons of olive oil. Toss the peppers and onions until thoroughly coated and place into a hot raised-grill sauté pan. Cook for about 3 minutes then remove the peppers and onion from the pan and set aside.

In a freestanding mixer or hand mixer, blend the butter on a medium speed until smooth. Then add the feta cheese, chopped garlic, cracked black pepper and fresh chives into the smooth butter and continue blending until once again smooth. When the butter is ready, it is time to assemble the parchments. Spray the piece of parchment paper with cooking spray before assembly.

The order of the assembly is:

A bed of fresh spinach leaves

Next the cooked lemon couscous

Six shrimp

Half of the lobster meat in each parchment, some tail and a claw

Three cleaned mussels

The grilled peppers and onions

The Roma tomatoes

A "healthy" scoop of the feta cheese-chive butter

Place in a preheated 375-degree oven and bake for about 30 minutes. Remove from oven and serve, usually with some fresh lemon and some crusty French bread.

Traditional Beef
Tenderloin in a Wellington
Style, served with
Béarnaise Sauce
see recipe on
page 154

Roasted Veal "Osso Bucco" served
in a White Bean and Ham Hock Stew with Creamed
Anna Potatoes and Crusty French Bread
see recipe on page 166

Fresh Monkfish, Sea Scallops and Mussels Baked in Parchment Paper with Cheddar Cheese Grits, Collard Greens, Grilled Sweet Onions, Tomatoes, Surry Bacon and Tasso Ham Butter

. . . .

YIELD: 4 SERVINGS

INGREDIENTS:

6 tablespoons butter, softened

¼ cup finely diced Tasso ham

2 pounds fresh collard greens, washed

½ cup water

½ teaspoon fresh ground black pepper

Pinch of sea salt or table salt

1 cup julienne red onions

2 tablespoons blended olive oil

Nonstick cooking spray

1½ cups cooked Cheddar Cheese Grits (see page 172)

¾ pound boneless, skinless fresh monkfish tail, cubed

¾ pound fresh sea scallops, 20 to 30 count, remove the rough tag

¾ pound shrimp, 21 count, shell removed, butterflied and cleaned

¾ cup finely diced Roma tomatoes

8 slices Surry bacon or your favorite, cooked

PROCEDURE:

The first item to make is the Tasso ham butter. Place the softened butter in a food processor and blend on a medium-low speed until smooth. When smooth, add the diced Tasso ham and continue blending until thoroughly combined. Set aside or refrigerate if not using immediately.

Next, place the cleaned collard greens in a large saucepan with the water, ground black pepper and a pinch of sea salt. Cook over a medium heat and stir constantly until the collards begin to wilt. Remove from the saucepan and strain all excess water. Let the collards stand in the strainer and continue to drain. When assembling parchments, the collards are the base of the parchment and should be as dry as possible.

In a dry sauté pan over medium-high heat, combine the red onions and olive oil and cook until the onions begin to caramelized and turn

TOOLS

. . . .

Measuring spoons and cup, cutting board, chef's knife, food processor small mixing bowl, strainer, large saucepan, sauté pan, tongs, large spoon, parchment paper and baking pan

brown. Remove from the pan and set-aside until assembly. Spray the parchment paper with cooking spray before assembly.

This assembly the order is:

The cooked collard greens

The cooked Cheddar Cheese Grits, a large spoon full

The monkfish cubes, spread out

Three to four sea scallops, spread out

Three shrimp, spread out

The diced tomatoes

The grilled sweet onions

Two slices of cooked bacon

A "healthy" scoop of the Tasso Ham Butter

Place the parchments on a baking pan into a preheated 375-degree oven and bake for 30 minutes. Remove from the oven and serve immediately. Some side dish suggestions would be Cajun sour cream and warm corn bread.

Key Lime Tart served with Raspberry Sauce,
Toasted Coconut, Whipped Cream and Fresh Mint
see recipe on page 213

"Mudge Pie" served with Chocolate Sauce,
Whipped Cream and Fresh Mint
see recipe on page 212

After all these years, "still the best service in town."

Fresh Pompano, Lump Crabmeat and Mussels Baked in Parchment Paper with Creamy Rice, Grilled Sweet Bell Peppers, Cherry Tomatoes and Lemon-Lime Butter

. . . .

YIELD: 6 SERVINGS

INGREDIENTS:

½ pound butter (2 sticks), softened

Zest and juice of 2 lemons and 2 limes

1 cup red, yellow and green bell peppers, cut into thin strips

2 tablespoons olive oil

Salt and pepper

½ cup dry white rice

1½ cups chicken stock

¼ cup heavy cream

1 tablespoon butter

Nonstick cooking spray

6 (6-ounce) skinless pompano fillets

12 ounces jumbo lump crabmeat, picked free of shell

18 fresh mussels in the shell, washed and beards removed

1 pint cherry tomatoes, cut in halves

PROCEDURE:

In a freestanding mixer place the softened butter and the zest and juice from the lemons and limes. Blend on a medium speed until smooth. Remove the lemon-lime butter from the mixer and refrigerate until needed.

In a small mixing bowl toss the bell peppers with the olive oil, salt and pepper. On a hot grill or raised cast iron skillet cook the peppers until charred on the outside but still crisp. Remove from the grill and set aside. In a saucepan place the white rice and chicken stock and cook over a medium-high heat until the rice has absorbed the stock and is fork tender. Remove the rice from the saucepan and into a mixing bowl, then fold in the heavy cream and one tablespoon of butter. Let the creamy rice set at room temperature until needed. Stir occasionally.

TOOLS

. . . .

Measuring spoons and cup, cutting board, chef's knife, freestanding mixer, two rubber spatula, two small mixing bowls, zester and juicer, grill or raised skillet, raised-edge baking dish, saucepan wooden spoon, large spoon and baking pan.

It is time to assemble the parchments. Spray the entire inside surface of the parchment paper with the cooking spray.

The order of assemble is:

    A large scoop of the creamy rice on the bottom

    The fillet of pompano, spread out

    About two ounces of lump crabmeat

    Three mussels

    A generous amount of the grilled sweet bell peppers

    A generous amount of cherry tomato halves

    About two ounces of the lemon-lime butter

Place the parchments in a preheated 375-degree oven for approximately 30 minutes and serve with a small salad vinaigrette and crusty French bread.

My two girls, Casey and Kelly, wearing their Berret's t-shirts. Only a Chef-Dad could understand the feeling when Kelly says, "I don't want to go out to eat. I want Daddy's cooking."

The Berret's Family

Bottom row, left to right,
Tom Austin, Patrick Hilton, Richard Carr,
Randy Warren, Phyllis Allen, Bill Erwin

Top row, left to right,
Paul Wright, Pam Groman, Vinny Gaeta,
Mike Kellum, Lisa Hope, Thomas Greene, Don Haley, Maria Strong,
"Smitty," Terry Gallagher, Jen Austin

Sesame-Crusted Salmon Fillet and Shrimp Baked in Parchment Paper with Baby Spinach, Carrots, "Nutty" Rice, Grilled Sweet Onions, Tomatoes and Orange Butter

. . . .

YIELD: 4 SERVINGS

INGREDIENTS:

8 tablespoons butter (1 stick), softened

Zest and juice of 2 oranges

1 large sweet red onion, julienne cut and grilled or roasted

1 tablespoon olive oil

Salt and pepper

4 (5-ounce) salmon fillets

Nonstick cooking spray

2 tablespoons black sesame seeds

2 tablespoons white sesame seeds

¼ pound baby spinach leaves

1½ cups Seasoned "Nutty" Rice (see page 179)

16 shrimp, 21 count, shell and tail removed, butterflied and deveined

½ cup fresh carrots, cut into three-inch matchsticks

½ cup finely diced fresh Roma tomatoes

PROCEDURE:

In a freestanding mixer place the softened butter and the zest and juice of the two oranges. On medium speed blend the butter until smooth. Remove the orange butter from the mixer and refrigerate until needed.

Next, take the thin cut red onions and toss with olive oil, salt and pepper. On a hot grill, or a roasting pan in a 450-degree oven, cook the onions until browned and tender. Remove from the heat and set aside at room temperature.

Spray the salmon fillets with the cooking spray, then lightly coat with the salt, pepper and sesame seeds on both sides.

It is time to assemble the parchments. Spray the entire inside surface of the parchment paper with the cooking spray.

> ### TOOLS
> . . . .
>
> *Measuring spoons and cup, cutting board, chef's knife, freestanding mixer, roasting pan, rubber spatula and metal spoons.*

Sesame-Crusted Salmon Fillet and Shrimp continued

The order of assembly is.

A bed of the baby spinach leaves

A healthy scoop of the "Nutty" Rice

The sesame-crusted salmon, spread out

Four shrimp around the salmon

The carrots

The tomatoes

The grilled onions

About two to three tablespoons of the orange butter

Place the parchments in a preheated 375-degree for approximately 30 minutes. Additional serving suggestions could be a side of soy sauce, Wasabi or "hot" mustard sauce.

Fresh Sea Scallops and Shrimp Baked in Parchment Paper with Spinach, Rainbow Penne Pasta, Matchstick Carrots, Spring Onions and Roasted Roma Tomato-Garlic Butter

. . . .

YIELD: 6 SERVINGS

INGREDIENTS:

½ pound fresh Roma tomatoes, cut in halves

2 tablespoons olive oil

1 tablespoon finely chopped garlic

1 teaspoon cracked black pepper

1 teaspoon salt

8 tablespoons butter (1 stick), softened

Nonstick cooking spray

½ pound fresh spinach, stems removed

1 pound rainbow penne pasta, cooked, cooled and lightly oiled

2 pounds shrimp, 16 to 20 count, shell and tail removed, butterflied and cleaned

1½ pounds sea scallops, 20 count, tags removed

2 cups fresh carrots, cut into julienne strips

½ cup finely diced fresh spring onions

PROCEDURE:

In a small mixing bowl place the cut Roma tomatoes, olive oil, chopped garlic clove, black pepper and salt. Toss the tomatoes until thoroughly coated and place on a baking pan in a preheated 225-degree oven for about 45 minutes. Remove from the oven and set aside to cool at room temperature. In a freestanding or hand mixer, blend the butter on medium speed until smooth. Then add the roasted Roma tomatoes and garlic drippings to the smooth butter. Continue blending until the roasted tomatoes are thoroughly incorporated into the butter. Remove the tomato-garlic butter from the mixing bowl and refrigerate until needed. When the butter is ready, it is time to assemble the parchments. Spray the inside of the parchment paper with cooking spray before assembly.

TOOLS
. . . .
Measuring spoons and cup, cutting board, chef's knife, small mixing bowl, rubber spatula, baking pan, freestanding mixer and large spoon or scoop.

Fresh Sea Scallops and Shrimp continued

The order of the assembly is:

A bed of fresh spinach leaves

The cooked penne pasta

Six shrimp

Five to six sea scallops

The matchstick carrots

The spring onions

A "healthy" scoop of the tomato-garlic butter

Place the parchments in a preheated 375-degree oven and bake for 30 minutes. Remove from oven and serve immediately. A couple of side dishes would be grated Parmesan cheese and some crusty French bread.

Fresh Red Snapper Fillet, Littleneck Clams and Calamari Baked in Parchment Paper with Fettuccini, Spinach, Roma Tomatoes, Calamata Olives, Sweet Red Onions, Feta Cheese and Herb Vinaigrette Dressing

. . . .

YIELD: 6 SERVINGS

INGREDIENTS:

½ pound fresh Roma tomatoes, halved

1 cup sweet red onions, cut into thin strips

2 tablespoons halved pitted Calamata olives

1 cup House Herb Balsamic Vinaigrette Dressing (see page 49)

Nonstick cooking spray

½ pound fresh spinach, stems removed

½ pound fettuccini, cooked, cooled and lightly oiled

6 (5-ounce) skinless fresh red snapper fillets, rinsed and dried with paper towels

18 littleneck clams, washed well

1 pound cleaned squid tubes, sliced into ⅛-inch thick rings (see HINT)

½ pound feta cheese, crumbled

> ### HINT
> . . . .
> *For easy cutting, placed squid tubes in the freezer until solid then removed and slice.*

PROCEDURE:

In a small mixing bowl, place the cut Roma tomatoes, sweet red onions, Calamata olives and Herb Vinaigrette Dressing and toss all the ingredients until thoroughly coated. It is time to assemble the parchment. Remember to spray the inside piece of the parchment paper with cooking spray before assembly.

> ### TOOLS
> . . . .
> *Measuring spoons and cup, cutting board, chef's knife, small mixing bowl, rubber spatula, baking pan and large spoon.*

The order of the assembly is:

A bed of fresh spinach leaves

The cooked fettuccini

The red snapper fillet, spread out

Three littleneck clams

The squid rings

The feta cheese

The marinated tomatoes, red onions and olives

Pour the excess vinaigrette over the top

Place the parchments in a preheated 375-degree oven and bake for 30 minutes. Remove the parchments from oven and serve immediately. A couple of side dishes would be a small salad and some grilled flat bread drizzled with olive oil.

Baking in Parchment

On a piece of parchment paper cut to a twenty four by twelve inch rectangle spray the entire surface with an non-stick cooking spray. By visually centering the area on one half of the paper place the food is the order of assembly. This will allow the second half to be able to fold over the top of the assembled foods.

Fold the top half of the paper over the assembled foods and gently press down to let as much air as possible to be released.

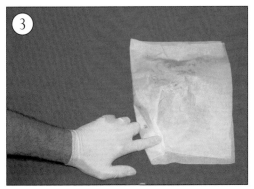

In the back closed end of the paper, closest to you make the first fold by pointing your fore finger towards to center of the food and making the fold over to seal.

By doing a fold on a curved one and half inch series, making sure each seal is covered to the next and always aiming at the center of the parchment paper.

Continue the fold until the circular motion is complete and the parchment is sealed.

On the final seal tuck the remaining paper underneath the completed folds to complete the seal of "Seafood baked in Parchment Paper."

MEAT ENTRÉES

MEAT ENTRÉES

Grilled Filet Mignon, 153

Traditional Beef Tenderloin, 154

Marsala Wine Seared Duck Breasts and Grilled Surry Sausage, 156

Herb-Crusted New Zealand Lamb Rack, 158

Roasted Leg of Lamb, Thick-Sliced, 160

Pistachio-Crusted Pork Loin, 162

Herb-Crusted French-Cut Veal Chop, 164

Roasted Veal "Osso Bucco", 166

Grilled Filet Mignon topped with Warm Brie Cheese, served with "Berret's" Steak Sauce, Fresh Spinach, Creamed Anna Potatoes, Tomatoes and Tarragon-Radish Sour Cream

. . . .

YIELD: 6 SERVINGS

INGREDIENTS:

6 (7-ounce) fully-trimmed filet mignons

2 tablespoons olive oil

1 tablespoon Montreal seasoning

6 (1-ounce) wedges Brie cheese

1 tablespoon white wine

1 pound fresh spinach leaves, stems removed

Salt and pepper

1 tablespoon butter, unsalted

¾ cup "Berret's" Steak Sauce (see page 202)

6 servings Creamed Anna Potatoes (see page 174)

¼ cup finely diced fresh Roma tomatoes

¼ cup Tarragon-Radish Sour Cream (see page 71)

6 sprigs fresh rosemary

PROCEDURE:

Rub the filet mignons with the olive oil and Montreal seasoning and place on a hot grill over medium heat. Cook the steaks until the serving temperature is reached then remove from the grill and let rest at room temperature. If the meat is cut before resting, the juices and flavor will run out. To finish the steaks, place in a preheated 375-degree oven with a wedge of Brie cheese on top of each and bake for about three minutes until the Brie cheese begins to melt.

While the steaks are finishing, place a large sauté pan over medium heat and add the white wine, spinach, salt and pepper. Stir the spinach as it wilts in the pan and just before it is completely wilted add the butter. Turn the heat off and coat the spinach with the butter.

It is time to "Plate-Up." On the bottom half of the plate, place a two-ounce pool of the Berret's Steak Sauce and then the Brie-cheese topped filet mignon on top of the sauce. Now, place a generous amount of the Creamed Anna Potatoes at the top of the plate and arrange the butter-wilted spinach next to the steak. Lastly, sprinkle the diced Roma tomatoes around the plate and place a tablespoon of the Tarragon-Radish Sour Cream on top of the melted Brie cheese. Garnish with the fresh rosemary sprigs.

TOOLS

. . . .

Measuring spoons and cup, cutting board, chef's knife, grill, metal turner, tongs, baking pan, sauté pan and ladle.

Traditional Beef Tenderloin in a Wellington Style, served with Béarnaise Sauce

YIELD: 8 TO 10 SERVINGS

INGREDIENTS:

1 whole beef tenderloin (see HINT)

2 tablespoons olive oil

3 tablespoons Montreal seasoning

3 tablespoons blended olive oil

1 large yellow onion, finely diced

1 tablespoon dried thyme leaves

2 tablespoons chopped garlic

1 pound shiitake mushroom caps, julienne

6 ounces boneless, skinless chicken breasts, cubed

2 egg whites (reserve yolks for the pastry)

Salt and ground black pepper

1 cup flour

1 (12x20-inch) sheet puff pastry

2 cups Béarnaise Reduction

2 cups Hollandaise Sauce (see page 190)

INGREDIENTS: *(for the Béarnaise Reduction)*

2 tablespoons fresh tarragon leaves, chopped fine

2 tablespoons white wine

1 tablespoon tarragon vinegar

2 tablespoons shallots, chopped fine

½ teapoon cracked black pepper

HINT

To prepare a whole beef tenderloin: Clean the tenderloin and remove the silver skin. The top end or large end of the tenderloin should be trimmed down until even with rest of the loin. The bottom of the loin or tail should be trimmed, then folded under the tenderloin. This should produce a very even loin to roll, cook and serve. Keep all the meat trimmings to be used in the stuffing or forcemeat.

PROCEDURE:

Rub the beef tenderloin with 2 tablespoons of olive oil and the Montreal seasoning and place in a large skillet or sauté pan. Sear on all sides to seal in the juices. Remove from the pan and set aside at room temperature to cool. In another sauté pan over medium-high heat, place the three tablespoons of blended olive oil, onions and thyme leaves. Cook until the onions begin to turn brown and caramelize. Add the chopped garlic and shiitake mushrooms and cook until the garlic is roasted and the mushrooms begin to turn limp. Remove the onion-mushroom mixture from the heat and place in a large mixing bowl.

In a food processor, place the raw chicken breast cubes and the reserved beef tenderloin scraps. Blend on a high speed until a meat

TOOLS

Measuring spoons and cup, cutting board, chef's knife, two large sauté pans, tongs, rubber spatula, large mixing bowl, food processor, rolling pin, large spoon, pastry brush, large baking pan, serrated knife and ladle.

paste is formed, then add the egg whites to the paste and blend again until smooth. In a large mixing bowl, combine the meat paste, salt, pepper and sautéed shiitake mushroom mixture and mix until thoroughly combined. This will make the stuffing or filling surrounding the tenderloin in the puff pastry.

On a countertop, sprinkle a handful of flour onto a rolling surface. Place the puff pastry sheet on the floured countertop and sprinkle with some additional flour. Using a standard rolling pin, begin to roll out the puff pastry to a wider and longer shape. After rolling, the width of the puff pastry sheet should be about 30 inches and the length about 18 inches. The size of the trimmed tenderloin will dictate the size of the puff pastry. Remember, like wrapping a Christmas present, it is better to be able to trim away excess than to come up short. The similarities continue with the centering and wrapping of the present.

In the center of the pastry, spread a generous amount of the stuffing, lengthwise. Now, place the seared tenderloin on top of the stuffing area of the puff pastry. Gently push the tenderloin down on to stuffing, leaving about ½ inch of stuffing along the length of the puff pastry beneath the tenderloin. Next, take the remaining stuffing and coat the exposed sides of the tenderloin with an even layer.

It is time to wrap the Wellington. First, take the closest side of the pastry and lay it over the top of the tenderloin. Second, mix the reserved egg yolks with a little water and brush the top of the puff pastry. The egg mix acts as a glue to help seal the package. Third, bring the other side of the puff pastry over the top of the tenderloin to seal the tenderloin package. Gently turn the pastry-wrapped tenderloin on its side and trim the edges. Tuck the sides in, brush lightly with the egg-water mixture and create a sealed package.

Place the Wellington on a lightly greased or parchment-covered baking pan. Make a few small holes on the top of the pastry to allow steam to release and prevent the pastry from cracking during cooking. Place in a preheated 400-degree oven and bake for 25 minutes. This should allow enough time to brown the puff pastry, cook the stuffing and have tenderloin at a medium-rare serving temperature.

This would be a good time to make the Béarnaise Reduction. In a saucepan place the fresh tarragon, white wine, tarragon vinegar, shallots and cracked black pepper and place over a medium heat. The object is reduce the liquids into the tarragon and shallots until all of the liquid has been absorbed. When this has been accomplished, remove from the heat and let rest at room temperature. When the reduction has cooled, add into the Hollandaise Sauce and stir until thoroughly incorporated.

After removing from the oven, let rest for at least five minutes. To serve, place a small pool of Béarnaise Sauce on the plate. Using a serrated knife or electric knife, cut the Wellington into 1½ inch thick slices. Place on top of the Béarnaise Sauce and garnish with some fresh vegetables and a little more sauce. Serve with some crusty French bread and a small Caesar salad.

Marsala Wine Seared Duck Breasts and Grilled Surry Sausage served over Sour Cream, Garlic and Chive Smashed Potatoes with Baby French Green Beans, Crusty Bread and Champagne Onions

. . . .

YIELD: 6 SERVINGS

INGREDIENTS:

Nonstick cooking spray

2 sweet red onions, sliced very thin

½ cup champagne

6 (6-ounce) skinless double breasts of duck

2 tablespoons Montreal seasoning

½ cup flour

¼ cup blended olive oil

½ cup Marsala wine

1 cup Demi-Glace (see page 188)

12 (2-ounce) links Surry sausage

6 large slices French bread, bias cut

2 tablespoons extra virgin olive oil

6 servings Sour Cream and Chive Smashed Yukon Gold Potatoes (see page 177)

1 pound baby French green beans, blanched in lightly salted water

PROCEDURE:

Spray a sauté pan with the cooking spray. Add the thin slices of red onion and cook over a medium heat. When the onions begin to sear, add half of the champagne and let sizzle. When the onions have absorbed the first champagne add the rest and cook until the onions become limp and sweet. Remove from the heat and set-aside until "Plate-Up."

To start the duck breasts, season both sides with the Montreal seasoning and then dredge through the flour. In a hot sauté pan over medium-high heat, in the blended olive oil, place the floured duck breasts into the hot oil. While searing the breasts, reduce the heat to medium and turn often. This will ensure an even cooking temperature throughout the duck breasts. When the breasts are cooked to about medium, add the Marsala wine and set a match to the wine. When setting a flame to any pan, remove the pan from any open flame before igniting. This will prevent any uncontrolled flame. Remember, safety first in the kitchen. The alcohol will burn off retaining the flavor of the wine in the sauce. The combination of the wine, the flour from the duck breasts and Pomuse oil will start to make the Marsala wine sauce.

> ### TOOLS
> . . . .
> *Measuring spoons and cup, cutting board, chef's knife, two sauté pans, tongs, baking pan, ladle, metal turner and large spoon.*

Marsala Wine Seared Duck Breasts and Grilled Surry Sausage continued

When the flame goes out, add the Demi-Glace to the duck breast pan and stir to coat the meat. Reduce the heat to a simmer and continue coating the duck breast with the sauce. Place the Surry sausage links in a preheated 375-degree oven and cook for about five minutes. When the sausage links are just about done, place the bias-cut French bread, sprinkled with virgin olive oil, in the oven with the sausage to toast for the last minute.

Now let's "Plate-Up." Place a generous amount of the Sour Cream Smashed Potatoes in the center of the plate and then place the duck breasts leaning against the smashed potatoes. Lean the cooked sausage links against the potatoes and place the baby green beans around the duck breasts and potatoes. Pour the Marsala sauce over all the duck breasts and around the sausage links. Place the champagne onions on top of the duck breasts and serve with crusty French bread.

Herb-Crusted New Zealand Lamb Rack served with Rosemary Demi-Glace, Garlic-Smashed Potatoes and Sautéed Vegetables Ratatouille

· · · · · · · · · · · · · · · · · · · ·

YIELD: 4 SERVINGS

INGREDIENTS:

4 (1-pound) New Zealand lamb racks, French cut

1 tablespoon olive oil

2 tablespoons pureed or finely hand chopped fresh garlic, divided

Salt and black pepper

1 cup breadcrumbs

1 tablespoon dried thyme leaves

2 tablespoons finely chopped fresh rosemary, divided

¼ cup coarse ground mustard

8 medium Yukon gold potatoes, peeled and cooked in lightly salted water until fork tender

3 tablespoons butter

½ cup half-and-half cream

1 cup Demi-Glace (see page 188)

4 cups Ratatouille (see page 181)

1 dozen sprigs fresh rosemary

PROCEDURE:

To begin with, rub the lamb racks with the olive oil and 1 tablespoon garlic puree and season with salt and pepper. In a hot skillet over medium heat, place the lamb racks and sear on all sides. This has two purposes: to seal all the juices in the lamb rack as well as help quicken the final cooking time. Remove the seared lamb racks from the skillet and let rest at room temperature until cool.

In a mixing bowl, combine the breadcrumbs, thyme leaves and half the fresh rosemary to make the herb crusting. Next, cut the cooled lamb racks in half and with a pastry brush cover the lamb with the coarse ground mustard. Place the mustard-brushed lamb racks into the breading mixture and lightly coat the meat. Place the lamb racks on a pan in a preheated 375-degree oven for about 12 to 15 minutes. When the racks are ready, remove from the oven and let rest a couple of minutes before service.

To finish the potatoes, place the cooked Yukon gold potatoes into a saucepan with the butter, one tablespoon of garlic puree and

TOOLS

· · · · · · · · · · · ·

Measuring spoons and cup, cutting board, chef's knife, skillet, pastry brush, small mixing bowl, two saucepans, sauté pan, large spoon and ladle.

cream. On a medium-low heat, smash the potatoes with a fork, or other favorite utensil, and season with salt and pepper. Cook until hot.

The Demi-Glace should be placed in a small saucepan over a low heat with 1 tablespoon of the fresh rosemary. With the Ratatouille hot, it should be time to "Plate-Up." In the center of the plate, place a generous amount of the potatoes and Ratatouille and then ladle a pool of Demi-Glace around the potatoes and Ratatouille. The halved lamb racks should be placed facing each other, letting the bones fold together. It should resemble hands praying. Center the lamb racks on the potatoes and Ratatouille and garnish with fresh rosemary sprigs.

Roasted Leg of Lamb, Thick-Sliced and served with Creamy Mushroom Risotto, Demi-Glace, Spring Asparagus and Tomatoes

. . . .

YIELD: 8 TO 10 SERVINGS

INGREDIENTS:

1 whole leg of lamb (see HINT)

12 individual garlic cloves, peeled

½ cup pureed or finely hand chopped fresh garlic

½ cup pureed or finely hand chopped fresh shallot

½ cup olive oil

½ cup coarsely chopped fresh rosemary leaves

¼ cup coarse ground mustard

2 tablespoons cracked black pepper

2 tablespoons salt

6 servings Creamy Mushroom Risotto (see page 182)

1½ cups Demi-Glace (see page 188)

4 vine-ripened tomatoes, thinly sliced

1 pound fresh asparagus, peeled and lightly blanched in salt water

HINTS

. . . .

Ask the butcher for a "rolled, boned and tied" leg of lamb, also known as "RBT Lamb of Leg." This is by far the best piece of meat for roasting, stuffing and ease of slicing. I still believe there is a lot of romance in roasting a whole leg of lamb over an open spit; the leg of lamb hanging upside down and crackling over the fire. But in reality, in a conventional home kitchen, the romance may need to be at the candlelit table.

The average weight for the RBT leg of lamb ranges between 4 and 7 pounds. This recipe will be based on an average leg of lamb at 6 pounds. The cooking time should be based on internal temperature desired. For rare, about 120 degrees, medium at 140 degrees and well done at 160 degrees.

PROCEDURE:

Place the leg of lamb in a large raised-edge baking pan. Make a dozen one-inch slits in the meat around the leg and place the individual garlic cloves into the slits as deeply as possible. In

TOOLS

. . . .

Measuring spoons and cup, cutting board, chef's knife, roasting pan, mixing bowl, meat thermometer, carving knife and ladle.

a mixing bowl, place the pureed garlic and shallots, olive oil, chopped fresh rosemary and coarse ground mustard. Whisk together to form a paste. Rub the lamb leg with cracked black pepper and salt then pour the garlic-olive oil paste over the leg of lamb and coat completely.

Roasted Leg of Lamb continued

Place the leg of lamb into a preheated 375-degree oven for about 90 minutes, depending upon the size of the leg.

When the leg is done cooking, remove and let rest for at least 20 minutes before slicing. Cutting the meat too early would release all the juices.

When ready to serve, place a generous amount of the Creamy Mushroom Risotto at the top of the plate and ladle about two ounces of Demi-Glace on the bottom of the plate. Now, with a serrated or electric knife, cut the lamb in ½-inch slices and place on top of the sauce. To finish, lay the thinly sliced tomato and warm blanched asparagus alongside the risotto and serve.

Pistachio-Crusted Pork Loin served with Coarse Ground Mustard Sauce, Warm Sweet Red Cabbage Slaw and Red Bliss Potatoes

. . . .

YIELD: 4 SERVINGS

INGREDIENTS:

1 cup breadcrumbs

2 cups fine ground cracker meal

½ cup shelled pistachios

2 whole eggs

1 pint whole milk

8 (3-ounce) thinly sliced boneless pork loins

Salt and black pepper

¼ cup coarse ground mustard

½ cup blended olive oil

2 cups shredded red cabbage

2 tablespoons sugar

2 tablespoons salad oil

2 tablespoons apple cider vinegar

2 tablespoons raisins

¾ cup Coarse Ground Mustard Sauce (see page 193)

12 whole red bliss potatoes, peeled and blanched in lightly salted water until fork tender

PROCEDURE:

In a food processor, grind the breadcrumbs, cracker meal and pistachios into a smooth breading. In a mixing bowl, combine the eggs and milk to make an egg wash. Pound the pork loins with a meat mallet until as thin as possible. Season the pork with salt and pepper and brush with the coarse ground mustard on both sides. Dip the mustard-coated cutlets in the egg wash and then into the pistachio crusting. Coat thoroughly on both sides and set aside.

In a large sauté pan, place about half of the olive oil over a medium heat. When hot, place the breaded cutlets into the oil and cook about two minutes on each side until golden brown. Repeat this process to finish cooking all the pork.

TOOLS

. . . .

Measuring spoons and cup, cutting board, chef's knife, food processor, brush, two mixing bowls, whisk, two sauté pans, tongs, metal spatula and ladle.

To prepare the red cabbage slaw, take a large mixing bowl and add the shredded red cabbage, sugar, salad oil, cider vinegar and raisins, mixing thoroughly. To warm the red cabbage slaw, heat a dry sauté pan over medium heat and pour in the slaw. Stir until warm and limp.

In a small saucepan, heat the mustard sauce until warm. The red bliss potatoes should be hot. Now, it is time to "Plate-Up." In the center of the plate, place about two ounces of the coarse ground mustard sauce. Next, off the center of the plate, place the warm red cabbage slaw. On top of the sauce and slaw place two slices of the pistachio-crusted pork loin and finish with a few red bliss potatoes.

Herb-Crusted French-Cut Veal Chop served over Sun-Dried Cherry Demi-Glace with Seasoned Rice, Grilled Asparagus and Sweet Peppers

. . . .

YIELD: 6 SERVINGS

INGREDIENTS:

1 pound fresh asparagus, peeled and blanched in lightly salted water

Olive oil for drizzling

Salt and cracked black pepper

1 medium-sized sweet red bell pepper, julienne

¼ cup coarse ground mustard

2 tablespoons pureed or finely hand chopped shallots

2 tablespoons pureed or finely hand chopped fresh garlic

¼ cup olive oil

1 cup coarse ground breadcrumbs

¼ cup flour

¼ cup medium-grind cracker meal

1 tablespoon finely chopped fresh rosemary

1 teaspoon dried basil leaves

½ teaspoon dried oregano leaves

6 (12-ounce) bone-in veal chops

2 ounces sun-dried cherries

1 teaspoon sweet butter

2 ounces port wine

1½ cups Demi-Glace (see page 188)

3 cups Seasoned "Nutty" Rice (see page 179)

PROCEDURE:

Drizzle the asparagus with olive oil and season with salt and cracked black pepper. Lightly drizzle olive oil over the red bell pepper. Grill asparagus and bell pepper over an open grill or in a raised-edge cast iron skillet.

In a small mixing bowl, place the coarse ground mustard, shallots, garlic and ¼ cup olive oil. Mix well to make the wet rub of the breading sequence. In a second mixing bowl, combine the breadcrumbs, flour, cracker meal, fresh rosemary and dried herbs to make the dry portion of the breading sequence. Now brush the veal chops heavily with the wet mustard rub and then coat lightly with the herb breading. When the chops are ready, place on a lightly oiled baking pan and into a preheated 375-degree oven for about 20 minutes. The cooking time will also depend on the thickness of the chop.

TOOLS:
. . . .

Measuring spoons and cup, raised-edge cast iron skillet, cutting board, chef's knife, two mixing bowls, two saucepans, two whisks, wooden spoon, ladle, large spoon, baking dish, tongs and metal turner.

While the chops are cooking, in a small saucepan, place the dried cherries, butter and port wine over a medium heat. When the cherries start to plump up, add the Demi-Glace and reduce the heat to a simmer until time of service. The seasoned rice should already be hot and ready to serve. At the last minute, reheat the asparagus and sweet red bell peppers and it is time to "Plate-Up." First, take a healthy scoop of the seasoned rice and place at the top of the plate. Ladle the Demi-Glace at the bottom of the plate. Then place the chop on top of the Demi-Glace leaning on the seasoned rice. Next, arrange the grilled asparagus and sweet peppers resting against the rice and chop.

Roasted Veal "Osso Bucco" served in a White Bean and Ham Hock Stew with Creamed Anna Potatoes and Crusty French Bread

. . . .

YIELD: 6 SERVINGS

This is quite possibly my all-time favorite meat dish. Chef Rolf Tinner first introduced me to this dish as an apprentice and I have used this cooking method on various other pieces of meat as well as mushrooms and garlic.

INGREDIENTS:

6 pounds bone-in veal shanks, cross-cut against the bone

2 tablespoons Montreal seasoning

½ cup flour

½ cup blended olive oil

¼ cup hand chopped garlic

½ cup finely diced shallots

2 tablespoons dried thyme leaves

1 cup white wine

2 cups dried navy beans

3 smoked ham hocks

3 quarts chicken stock, low-sodium please

1 tablespoon crushed red pepper flakes

¼ cup apple cider vinegar

2 large carrots, finely diced

1 bunch celery, cut on a bias

2 medium-sized yellow onions, finely diced

6 servings Creamed Anna Potatoes (see page 174)

½ cup finely diced fresh Roma tomatoes

½ cup finely diced spring or green onions

6 thick-cut, large slices French bread, buttered and toasted

PROCEDURE:

To start, take the veal shanks, season with Montreal seasoning and lightly dust with flour. In a very hot skillet, place the blended olive oil and veal shanks. Sear on all sides to seal in the juices, remove from the skillet and set aside. In a roasting pan, place the chopped garlic, shallots, thyme leaves and the rendered oil from the hot skillet. Place the roasting pan in a preheated 375-degree oven and cook for about 10 minutes until the shallots and garlic are browned and tender. Take the pan from the oven and add the white wine to the pan, stirring constantly to get all the juices and flavors from the bottom of the pan.

> ### TOOLS
> . . . .
> *Measuring spoons and cup, cutting board, chef's knife, skillet, metal turner, tongs, large roasting pan, large spoon, baking pan and large ladle.*

Roasted Veal "Osso Bucco" continued

Now, place the veal shanks into the roasting pan and add the navy beans, ham hocks, chicken stock, crushed red pepper flakes and vinegar. Combine all the ingredients, cover with foil and place in a preheated 325-degree oven for about 2 hours.

After 2 hours, your house smells great and everyone's getting hungry. Remove the veal shanks from the oven and uncover. Add the carrots, celery and onions and stir the vegetables into the bean mixture. Re-cover the pan and let rest. After about 20 minutes, uncover the pan and remove the ham hocks. To flake the meat from the ham hocks into the stew, remove the outside fat, pull the meat off the bone and add the meat back to the white bean stew. Save the bone for the dogs.

It is now time to "Plate-Up." This dish should be served in a very large bowl or rimmed plate. First, take a large portion of the Creamed Anna Potatoes and place in the center of the bowl. Next, take a large ladle of the white bean-ham hock stew and pour around the potatoes. Set a large portion of the veal shank on top of the white beans and lean the meat against the potatoes. Sprinkle the dish with the fresh diced tomatoes and spring onions. Lastly, take the toasted and buttered French bread and place next to the potatoes.

SIDE DISHES
& SAUCES

· · · · · · · · · · · · · ·

SIDE DISHES
& SAUCES

Banana Nut Bread

. . . .

YIELD: ONE 18-INCH LOAF

INGREDIENTS:

½ pound butter (2 sticks), softened

1 cup sugar

4 whole extra large eggs

1 cup sliced very ripe bananas
   (about 3 bananas)

1½ cups all-purpose flour, sifted

¾ tablespoon baking soda

Pinch of salt

¼ cup crushed nuts of your choice, walnuts
   or pecans

Nonstick cooking spray

PROCEDURE:

In a freestanding mixer place the softened butter and sugar and blend on medium speed until a creamy texture is reached. Be sure to take a rubber spatula and scrape the paddle, sides and bottom of the bowl to make sure all of the butter-sugar is incorporated. Next, add the eggs one at a time, then the bananas, and continue to mix until thoroughly creamed.

In a separate mixing bowl place the flour, baking soda and salt, and stir until thoroughly combined. Reduce the speed on the mixer to medium-low and slowly add the flour ingredients to the liquid mixture. When the flour has been totally incorporated into the liquid mixture, turn the mixer off and scrape down the paddle, sides and bottom again. Mix the batter a minute or two more to ensure a smooth batter. Fold the nuts into the batter to spread throughout the bread.

Spray the loaf bread pan with the cooking spray and then sprinkle a little flour into the pan. Pour the bread batter evenly into the pan and smooth the top of the batter with a rubber spatula. Place the pan into a preheated 350-degree oven and bake for 30 to 40 minutes, rotating halfway through the cooking cycle. Test the cooked loaf with a toothpick after 30 minutes, and if the toothpick comes out clean, remove the bread from the oven. After removing from the oven, turn the bread out of the pan as quickly as possible and place on raised grill pan or bread cooling rack. The object is to ensure the proper airflow to circulate around the bread as it cools.

Let the cooked loaf rest at room temperature for about 30 minutes before slicing or serving.

> ## TOOLS
> . . . .
> *Measuring spoons and cup, rubber spatulas, loaf baking pan, mixer, resting grate, toothpick and chef's knife.*

Cheddar Cheese Grits

. . . .

YIELD: ABOUT 10 SERVINGS

INGREDIENTS:

6 cups chicken stock

8 ounces quick grits, Quaker is great!

1 pound sharp Cheddar cheese, grated

¼ pound Parmesan cheese, grated

1 teaspoon salt

1 teaspoon white pepper

PROCEDURE:

In a large saucepan bring the chicken stock to a low boil, add the quick grits, and continuously stir until thick. When the grits return to a boil remove from the heat and place into a freestanding mixer on a low speed. Next, add the grated Cheddar cheese, Parmesan cheese, salt and white pepper and continue to stir. When the cheeses are melted into the grits, remove from the mixer and taste. Season with more pepper, salt or cheese, and serve.

TOOLS

. . . .

Measuring spoons and cup, cutting board, saucepan, whisk, freestanding mixer, rubber spatula and box grater.

Using unprocessed grits is a great concept but don't bother unless you are willing to spend a lot of time and energy to gain the same product as quick grits provides. A true Southerner in Georgia would never buy a quick grits product, but then again, I was raised in Michigan and live in Virginia.

Sweet Corn Relish

YIELD: ABOUT 1 QUART

INGREDIENTS:

1 cup fresh white or yellow corn, shucked and taken off the cob

1 medium-sized sweet red onion, finely diced

2 medium-sized green bell peppers, finely diced

1 medium-sized red bell pepper, finely diced

2 spring onions, finely diced

¼ cup apple cider vinegar

¼ cup balsamic vinegar

¼ cup salad, canola, or soybean oil

½ teaspoon salt

3 tablespoons sugar

½ teaspoon crushed red pepper flakes

2 tablespoons chopped fresh parsley

PROCEDURE:

In a large mixing bowl place the corn, red onion, bell peppers and spring onion, and toss until thoroughly combined.

In a separate, smaller mixing bowl place the two vinegars, salad oil, salt, sugar, red pepper flakes and parsley. Whisk these ingredients together to make a vinaigrette dressing. Add the vinaigrette dressing to the vegetable mixture and gently toss together, then refrigerate for at least one hour before service.

TOOLS

Measuring spoons and cup, cutting board, chef's knife, two mixing bowls and wire whisk.

Creamed Anna Potatoes

· ·

YIELD: 6 TO 8 SERVINGS

INGREDIENTS:

2 quarts lightly salted water

2 pounds whole russet potatoes, peeled and
   sliced thick

2 tablespoons salt

1 tablespoon white pepper

½ teaspoon nutmeg

½ teaspoon garlic powder

½ teaspoon onion powder

½ cup shredded Parmesan cheese

1 cup heavy cream

PROCEDURE:

In a large saucepan over medium-high heat place the lightly salted water and potatoes. Bring to a boil, then reduce the heat to a simmer and cook the potatoes until they are fork tender. This means to be able to stick a fork through the potato without any resistance.

This is the "be gentle" stage. Pour the water off of the potatoes through a pasta strainer and carefully place the potatoes into a large mixing bowl and let rest. In a smaller mixing bowl, combine the salt, pepper, nutmeg, garlic powder and onion powder. After combining the seasonings, sprinkle into the standing potatoes and gently toss until thoroughly seasoned. Be gentle, just toss the seasonings with the potatoes but do not mash or try to use a utensil. Now, take the seasoned, cooked potatoes and pour loosely into a casserole dish. Let the potatoes settle into the pan casually. Sprinkle the top of the potatoes with the shredded Parmesan cheese, and then pour the heavy cream evenly over the casserole. Lift the casserole dish and lightly bang down on the counter-top to allow some of the cream and cheese to go down throughout the potatoes.

In a preheated 375-degree oven, place the covered casserole dish and bake for about 15 minutes, remove from oven, and serve.

TOOLS

· · · · · · · · · · · · ·

Measuring spoons and cup, cutting board, chef's knife, large saucepan, pasta strainer, two mixing bowls, rubber spatula, whisk and covered casserole dish.

Berret's "Dirty Rice"

INGREDIENTS:

½ cup dry white rice

1½ cups chicken stock

2 pieces bacon, finely diced

¼ pound ground pork sausage

¼ cup finely diced yellow onion

¼ cup finely diced green bell pepper

1 tablespoon pureed or finely chopped fresh garlic

¼ teaspoon dried thyme leaves

½ teaspoon ground red pepper or cayenne

¼ teaspoon ground black pepper

Pinch of onion powder

Pinch of salt

1 tablespoon butter

2 tablespoons heavy cream

PROCEDURE:

In a saucepan place the white rice and chicken stock over a medium heat and cook until the rice has absorbed all of the stock. Remove the cooked rice from the heat and set aside.

In a large sauté pan, place the bacon and ground sausage and cook over a medium-high heat until the bacon is crispy and the sausage is completely cooked. Next, lower the heat to medium-low and add the onion, bell pepper, garlic, dried thyme and spices. Cook until the peppers and onions are tender, then add the cooked rice and stir until all the ingredients are thoroughly combined. Bring to a simmer and then fold in the butter and cream. The "Dirty Rice" is now read to serve.

TOOLS

Measuring spoons and cup, cutting board, chef's knife, saucepan, sauté pan or wok, wooden spoon, whisk and large spoon.

Garlic-Shallot Butter

. . . .

YIELD: ABOUT 1 POUND

This butter is a main stay in any kitchen. It is essential to have this butter made and ready whenever it is needed. This versatile butter is known by many names: Maitre De Hotel Butter, Scampi Butter, and Escargot Butter, to name a few.

INGREDIENTS:

1 pound of the finest butter, softened (see HINT)

¼ cup very finely chopped fresh parsley, stems removed

¼ cup very finely hand-chopped fresh shallots

¼ cup very finely hand-chopped fresh garlic (see HINT)

1 teaspoon lemon juice

1 tablespoon Worcestershire sauce

1 teaspoon whole black peppercorns, freshly ground

1 teaspoon Tabasco sauce

Pinch of salt

> ### HINTS
> . . . .
>
> *A sweet butter is preferred. A French Normandy butter or even a Vermont American butter would be wonderful. Do not use a food processor to puree the garlic as it will bruise the garlic and not allow the full flavor of the clove to be released.*

PROCEDURE:

Before the days of food processors, this butter was made through the meat grinding attachment of a mixer. Before then, it was made with a mortar and pestle. Now, in a freestanding mixer or food processor, place the softened butter on a low speed and beat until smooth. Next, add the parsley, shallots, garlic, lemon juice, Worcestershire sauce, pepper, Tabasco sauce and salt. Blend on a low speed until once again smooth. It is only necessary to blend this butter until smooth and the ingredients are evenly distributed. Please do not over-mix the butter as it will bruise the parsley and garlic. Refrigerate until duty calls.

> ### TOOLS
> . . . .
>
> *Measuring spoons and cup, cutting board, chef's knife, freestanding mixer, rubber spatula and spoon.*

Sour Cream and Chive
Smashed Yukon Gold Potatoes

. . . .

YIELD: 6 TO 8 SERVINGS

INGREDIENTS:

2 quarts lightly salted water

2 pounds Yukon gold potatoes, peeled and
    cut in quarters

¼ cup fresh garlic cloves, lightly salted

1 tablespoon salt

1 tablespoon white pepper

1 cup sour cream

½ cup heavy cream

¼ cup very thinly sliced fresh chives

PROCEDURE:

In a large saucepan place the lightly salted water and quartered potatoes and bring to a boil over medium-high heat. Once the potatoes have come to a boil, reduce the heat to a simmer and cook the potatoes until they are fork tender. This means to be able to stick a fork through the potato without any resistance.

While the potatoes are cooking, place the lightly salted garlic cloves in a preheated 375-degree oven and roast for about 6 minutes. The garlic cloves should be brown, caramelized and smell great. The intensity of the garlic clove changes to a sweet, nutty and roasted flavor.

When the potatoes are fork tender, pour the water off of the potatoes through a pasta strainer and place the potatoes in a large mixing bowl to rest. In a small mixing bowl combine the salt, pepper, sour cream, heavy cream, fresh chives and roasted garlic. Use a hand mixer to blend the ingredients as well as break up the roasted garlic cloves. Pour this creamy garlic mixture over the resting potatoes and use the hand mixture to smash the potatoes into lumpy mashed potatoes.

TOOLS

. . . .

Measuring spoons and cup, cutting board, chef's knife, large saucepan, pasta strainer, two mixing bowls, rubber spatula, whisk and hand mixer.

Pan-Fried Country Ham
and Cheddar Cheese Grit Cakes

YIELD: 6 TO 8 SERVINGS

INGREDIENTS:

5 cups water, lightly salted

1½ cups quick grits

½ cup fresh corn, cut off the cob

¼ cup country ham, shredded into small pieces

¼ cup grated Cheddar cheese

½ cup finely diced red bell pepper

Pinch of ground black pepper

¼ cup blended olive oil

Nonstick cooking spray

PROCEDURE:

In a saucepan over medium-high heat bring the lightly salted water to a boil, then add the quick grits and stir. Reduce the heat to a simmer and cook the grits until thick, stirring frequently so the grits do not stick to the pan. When the grits are cooked, remove from the saucepan and pour into a mixing bowl. Next, add the fresh kernel corn, country ham, Cheddar cheese, diced red bell pepper and ground black pepper. Fold all the ingredients together and pour into a rimmed baking pan sprayed with cooking spray. Refrigerate until cold.

When the grits are cold, cut with a cookie cutter into whatever shape cakes you desire. In a sauté pan over a medium heat, add the blended olive oil and, when hot, add the grit cakes. Pan fry the grit cakes for about two minutes on each side until crispy and serve.

TOOLS

Measuring spoons and cup, cutting board, chef's knife, covered saucepan, whisk, large mixing bowl, rubber spatula, rimmed baking dish, cookie cutters, sauté pan and metal turner.

Seasoned "Nutty" Rice

INGREDIENTS:

½ cup dry white rice

½ cup water

1 cup chicken stock

½ cup heavy cream

¼ cup shredded Parmesan cheese

¼ cup chopped salted peanuts

¼ cup finely diced fresh Roma tomatoes

1 teaspoon salt

1 teaspoon white pepper

PROCEDURES:

In a two-quart "covered" casserole dish combine the rice, water and chicken stock and place in a preheated 375-degree over for approximately 25 minutes. When the rice is cooked, remove the cover from the casserole dish and stir to make sure the rice has absorbed all of the liquid. Next, add the heavy cream and Parmesan cheese and stir until the cheese is melted and the cream is thoroughly mixed in. Then add the chopped peanuts, diced tomatoes, salt and white pepper, and stir until the rice has become a creamy, nutty, "risotto-type" rice. Cover the casserole and keep warm until time of service.

TOOLS

· · · · · · · · · · · · · ·

Measuring spoons and cup, cutting board, chef's knife, food processor, casserole dish and wooden spoon or rubber spatula.

A Pretty Traditional Pesto

YIELD: ABOUT ½ CUP

INGREDIENTS:

¼ pound fresh basil leaves
2 tablespoons pine nuts
¼ cup fresh garlic cloves
1 tablespoon grated Parmesan cheese

½ teaspoon whole black peppercorns, ground fine
¼ cup extra virgin olive oil
Pinch of salt

PROCEDURE:

Place the fresh basil leaves, pine nuts, garlic cloves, Parmesan cheese and cracked black pepper into a food processor. Blend on a medium speed until all the ingredients are thoroughly combined. Then reduce the speed to low and begin to drizzle the olive oil into the basil mixture, forming a paste. When finished adding the oil, let the pesto blend until thoroughly combined. Lastly, add a pinch of salt and continue blending to finish the pesto paste. Remove from the processor, wrap thoroughly and refrigerate until needed. It is important to wrap thoroughly because you do not want the entire refrigerator to smell like garlic. The shelf life in the refrigerator is about a month, but it can also be frozen for up to three months.

TOOLS

Measuring spoons and cup, cutting board, chef's knife, food processor and rubber spatula.

Ratatouille

INGREDIENTS:

1 cup blended olive oil, divided

2 tablespoons finely chopped fresh shallots

1 tablespoon pureed or finely hand-chopped fresh garlic

1 tablespoon dried thyme leaves

1 tablespoon dried basil leaves

1 tablespoon salt

1 tablespoon white pepper

1 cup diced yellow onion

2 cups diced yellow squash

2 cups diced zucchini

2 cups peeled and diced eggplant

1 cup diced fresh Roma tomatoes

½ cup grated Parmesan cheese

PROCEDURE:

In a large sauté pan place half of the blended olive oil on medium heat. When the oil is hot, add the chopped shallots and garlic puree. Cook the garlic and shallots until roasted brown, then reduce the heat to low and add the thyme, basil, salt and white pepper. Stir until thoroughly combined and then add the yellow onion, squash, zucchini and eggplant. Increase the heat to medium and continuously stir the vegetables until they have absorbed the hot garlic oil. Next, add the remaining olive oil and continue to stir the ratatouille until the vegetables are cooked, but still a little crunchy.

Finish the dish by adding the Roma tomatoes and Parmesan cheese, turn off the heat, stir, and cover. This should allow the cheese to melt, the tomatoes to incorporate into the dish, and everything to stay warm. Before serving, taste the ratatouille and adjust the salt and pepper if needed.

TOOLS

· · · · · · · · · · · · · ·

Measuring spoons and cup, cutting board, chef's knife, sauté pan, rubber spatula and large spoon.

Creamy Mushroom Risotto

· ·

YIELD: ABOUT 6 SERVINGS

INGREDIENTS:

½ cup dry Arborio rice

½ cup water

1 cup chicken stock

1 pound shiitake mushroom caps, sliced

¼ cup olive oil

1 tablespoon pureed or finely hand-chopped
   fresh garlic

½ cup heavy cream

½ cup finely diced fresh Roma tomatoes

½ pound unsalted butter (2 sticks), softened

1 teaspoon salt

1 teaspoon white pepper

PROCEDURES:

In a two-quart "covered" casserole dish combine the rice, water and chicken stock and place in a preheated 375-degree oven for approximately 25 minutes. When the rice is cooked, remove the cover from the casserole dish and stir to make sure the rice has absorbed all of the liquid.

In a sauté pan place the shiitake mushroom slices, olive oil and garlic puree, and cook until the mushrooms are limp and the garlic is roasted. Add the cooked mushrooms to the fully cooked rice and stir until thoroughly combined. Next, add the heavy cream, Roma tomatoes and sliced softened butter, and stir until the butter is melted and the cream is thoroughly mixed in. Season with the salt and white pepper and stir until the rice has become a creamy consistency, "risotto-type." Recover the casserole to keep warm until time of service.

TOOLS

· · · · · · · · · · · · · ·

Measuring spoons and cup, cutting board, chef's knife, sauté pan, covered casserole dish, and wooden spoon or rubber spatula.

Spoon Bread

YIELD: ABOUT 10 SERVINGS

INGREDIENTS:

¾ cup water, lightly salted
¾ cup half-and-half cream
1½ cups cornmeal
3 tablespoons sugar
4 tablespoons butter, softened

6 whole eggs
1 tablespoon baking powder
1 cup fresh kernel corn
Pinch of salt and white pepper
Nonstick cooking spray

PROCEDURE:

In a large saucepan bring the lightly salted water and half-and-half cream to a low boil. Add the cornmeal and return to a boil. Remove the thickened cornmeal from the heat, place in a large mixing bowl and add the sugar and butter. Mix the sugar and butter into the thickened cornmeal until smooth. In a separate mixing bowl, mix the eggs, baking powder, kernel corn and a pinch of salt and white pepper. When thoroughly combined, add the egg mixture to the thickened cornmeal and stir until a smooth batter forms.

In a sprayed casserole dish, pour the spoon bread batter and level the top for an even cooking surface. Place the casserole into a preheated 300-degree oven and bake for approximately 45 minutes. The clean toothpick test and a raised, cake-like center will prove the spoon bread is finished. Let the spoon bread rest before service. Do not be alarmed if the center falls in as the air is released.

TOOLS

Measuring spoons and cup, large saucepan, two large mixing bowls, two whips, rubber spatula, casserole dish and a toothpick.

Sweet Pepper Green Cabbage Slaw

YIELD: 8 SERVINGS

INGREDIENTS:

1 large head green cabbage, outer leaves removed

1 large yellow bell pepper, finely diced

1 large red bell pepper, finely diced

1 tablespoon salt

2 tablespoons salad oil

1 cup apple cider vinegar

¼ cup sugar

1 tablespoon dried oregano leaves

1 tablespoon ground black pepper

PROCEDURE:

Cut the head of cabbage in half, remove the core and cut into very thin slices or shredded on a box shredder. In a large mixing bowl place the shredded cabbage and the diced red and yellow bell peppers and sprinkle with the salt and salad oil. Toss the cabbage mixture until thoroughly coated and set aside.

In a small saucepan heat the apple cider vinegar with the sugar until the sugar has dissolved. Remove the vinegar from the heat and add the dry oregano leaves and ground black pepper. Now, pour the warm sweet vinegar over the cabbage mixture and toss until the vinegar dressing has thoroughly coated the green cabbage slaw. Refrigerate until time of service.

TOOLS

Measuring spoons and cup, cutting board, chef's knife, box grater, large mixing bowl, tongs, saucepan, whisk and rubber spatula.

Charred Tomato and Black Bean Relish

. . . .

YIELD: ABOUT 1 QUART

INGREDIENTS:

2 large ripe tomatoes, cored, grilled and cooled

½ large red onion, thick sliced, grilled and cooled

1 jalapeño pepper, trimmed, grilled and cooled

1 cup cooked black beans, cooled

1½ tablespoons white wine vinegar

1 teaspoon coarse ground mustard

1 teaspoon brown sugar

1 teaspoon fresh squeezed lime juice

½ teaspoon salt

½ teaspoon chili powder

¼ teaspoon ground chipotle powder or ground red pepper

¼ cup finely chopped cilantro

PROCEDURE:

The tomatoes, red onion and jalapeño pepper can be charred over an open grill or in an oven on broil. The needed result is to see some caramelization (burnt appearance) on the skin. In a food processor, coarse chop or pulse a few seconds at a time the tomatoes, red onions and jalapeño pepper. Please do not puree.

In a large mixing bowl place the cooked black beans, chopped tomato mixture, vinegar, mustard, sugar, lime juice, seasonings and cilantro. Now, stir gently until all the ingredients are thoroughly combined. Place in a refrigerator for at least 20 before serving.

TOOLS

. . . .

Measuring spoons and cup, cutting board, chef's knife, food processor, large mixing bowl and large spoon.

Caramel Sauce

YIELD: ABOUT 1 CUP

INGREDIENTS:

½ cup sugar
¼ cup water
1 teaspoon lemon juice
¼ cup heavy cream (see HINT)

> **HINT**
>
> *The substitution of butter in place of the cream would give you a caramel suitable for applications like apple dipping or candy making. Please remember the substitution of butter will not cool the caramelizing sugar as quickly as the cream, and the caramel should be removed from the heat earlier in the process.*

PROCEDURE:

In a cast iron skillet if you have one, or a sauté pan, place the sugar, water and lemon juice over a medium-high heat. The reason to use cast iron is a more even and intense heat. This will quicken the process. Bring the sugar-water to a rapid boil and stir constantly with a wooden spoon. The use of a wooden spoon will prevent the drawing of the heat out of the sauce while stirring. After a few minutes the sugar-water will begin to turn brown and caramelize.

Now, continue stirring until the color starts to reach a golden brown. Once the color crosses from golden brown to a deep brown color, remove from the heat and continue to stir constantly. This caramel sugar is now around 350 degrees and still cooking. To stop the cooking process, slowly drizzle the cream into the hot sugar mixture. Do not be alarmed at the first reaction of the caramel as the cream is slowly added. It will be similar to putting water on a fire, but the rise of steam and foam will only last a few seconds. The temperature will begin to reduce and cool the caramel as you continue to stir.

Serve when desired and refrigerate between uses. This caramel will last in your refrigerator for up to a month.

> **TOOLS**
>
> *Measuring spoons and cup, cast iron skillet or sauté pan, and wooden spoon.*

Chocolate Sauce

INGREDIENTS:

¼ pound dark semi-sweet chocolate or chocolate chips

3 tablespoons butter

½ cup heavy cream

½ teaspoon vanilla extract

½ cup confectioners' sugar

PROCEDURE:

In a double boiler, meaning not over direct heat, use a four- to six-quart saucepan filled about two-thirds of the way with hot water. On medium-high heat bring the water to a boil. In a six- to eight-quart mixing bowl, place the chocolate and butter over the boiling saucepan. A double boiler set-up will take longer to cook but will prevent the burning or scorching of the food. Let the chocolate-butter mixture melt, stirring frequently until the chocolate-butter is dissolved and very smooth. Next add the heavy cream and vanilla extract, reduce the heat to about medium-low, and stir until smooth. At this stage the chocolate should look similar to a large cup of hot chocolate. Lastly add the confectioners' sugar, a little at a time, until fully incorporated into the chocolate. Continue stirring until smooth.

Remove from the heat and serve when ready. When ready to refrigerate, place in a plastic container. In order to reheat, use the same double-boiler set-up or microwave on low. Do not thin down; this chocolate sauce will reheat to the same original consistency.

TOOLS

Measuring spoons and cup, four- to six-quart saucepan, six- to eight-quart mixing bowl, whip and rubber spatula.

Demi-Glace

YIELD: ABOUT 2 QUARTS

This sauce is one of the reasons why there is this book. I debated including a recipe for Demi-Glace, thinking who would actually make this at home. But just like baking bread from scratch, the purist realizes that after taking the time to make Demi-Glace from bones, you will never go back to a powder.

"The romance is back!"

INGREDIENTS:

10 pounds veal bones, leg bones only!

1 cup tomato paste

1 cup red wine

3 yellow onions, skin on

2 bunches celery, leaves removed, coarsely cut

2 gallons water

¼ cup finely chopped fresh garlic

3 bay leaves

¼ cup whole black peppercorns

2 tablespoons salt

3 tablespoons dried thyme leaves

PROCEDURE:

The process of making a Demi-Glace will take at least four hours. To get started, take the veal bones and rub with the tomato paste. Place in a preheated oven at 400 degrees for about 20 minutes or until the paste begins to caramelize black. At this point remove the bones from the pan and into a stockpot. Add the red wine to the pan the bones were roasted on and take a whisk or spoon and spread the wine around to remove all the burnt goodies from the pan. Then pour the wine and the goodies in the stockpot with the bones. The importance of using veal leg bones is significant for the natural gelatin that will thicken the Glace and fortify the flavor.

Cut the onions in half and place, cut-side down, on a hot skillet over medium-high heat until the onion flesh is burnt and smoky flavored. This is to caramelize the onion, which will give the roasted color and smoky flavor to this rich reduction sauce. Once the onions are caramelized, place in the stockpot along with the celery, water, garlic and spices. Over a medium-high heat bring to a boil, then reduce the heat to medium and let simmer for at least two hours.

TOOLS

· · · · · · · · · · · ·

Measuring spoons and cup, cutting board, chef's knife, roasting pan, pastry brush, whisk, spoon and stockpot.

Demi-Glace continued

After about two hours, half of the water will have evaporated and it is now time to strain the stock. Pour the stock through a china cap or mesh strainer to trap all the bones and debris. Take the time to make sure your stock is free of any debris. Double strain if necessary and discard the bones and vegetables. Place the strained stock into a fresh pot and return to the heat.

Now that you have Glace, bring the strained Glace to a low boil and let it reduce again to about half of that volume. Now you have Demi-Glace. The Demi-Glace will seem naturally thicken slightly. That is the consistency that the Demi-Glace should have. If the bones do not have enough gelatin to thicken the Demi-Glace, then it may be necessary to add a cornstarch-water thickening agent to the boiling stock. When doing so make sure the stock returns to a boil after introducing the thickening agent.

Remove the Demi-Glace and place in smaller metal containers and chill as quickly as possible. The use of an ice bath is the best method to chill quickly. Also take notice of the fact the cooled Demi-Glace will appear to take on a gelatinous consistency. When reheating do not add liquid to the Demi-Glace thinking that it is too thick, just reheat slowly.

Hollandaise Sauce

· ·

YIELD: 1½ CUPS

INGREDIENTS:

4 egg yolks

2 tablespoons lemon juice, fresh squeezed

1 teaspoon white vinegar

2 dashes of Tabasco sauce (optional)

¾ pound butter (3 sticks), melted, clarified
   and at room temperature (see HINT)

Pinch of salt and white pepper

PROCEDURE:

At home, I think the easiest way to make a Hollandaise Sauce is over a double boiler. What's a double boiler, you say? Fill a four-quart saucepan half full of water and bring to a rolling boil, then reduce the heat to medium. In an eight-quart mixing bowl place the eggs, lemon juice, vinegar and Tabasco sauce. Place the mixing bowl over the boiling water and whip the eggs until they start to become frothy and lighter in color. Remove the egg mixture from the heat and begin the emulsion stage. By slowly ladling the room temperature clarified butter into the egg mixture and whipping the entire time, you let the cooked eggs accept the butter and form an emulsion. The eggs and butter will begin to thicken as a sauce. Please do not add the butter any faster than you whip and always whip in the same direction. After all the butter has been incorporated into the eggs, add the salt and pepper. Now, taste the sauce and see if it needs any more lemon or Tabasco. Remember it is your sauce.

At this time add any variation you would like to the basic Hollandaise Sauce. Please serve this sauce immediately. This sauce is subject to bacteria and could be a health risk if not served quickly. Otherwise, it is one of the mother sauces and served responsibly should not pose any health risks.

> ### HINT
> · · · · · · · · · · · · · ·
> *Clarifying butter means to remove all the impurities from the melted butter. In a saucepan melt the butter completely over a medium heat until the butter is hot and golden in color. After the butter has reached a golden clear color remove the butter from the heat and pour into a clean room temperature metal container. The melted butter should rest. This will allow the impurities from the butter solids to settle to the bottom of the pan. Now, slowly pour the lighter clarified butter from the top of the pan into a clean new metal container and discard the remains from the original container.*
>
> *Options or variations on Hollandaise Sauce are endless. The traditional ones are Béarnaise or Maltaise. For any other fresh herb or ingredient desired, experiment but remember Hollandaise Sauce is basically a warm mayonnaise with a sensitive side.*

> ### TOOLS
> · · · · · · · · · · · · ·
> *One four-quart saucepan or pot, one eight-quart mixing bowl, wire whisk, measuring cup and spoons and ladle.*

Horseradish Cream Sauce

INGREDIENTS:

1 cup heavy cream

½ cube chicken or seafood bouillon

2 tablespoons sweet butter (unsalted), softened

3 tablespoons cream cheese, softened

2 tablespoons fresh grated or drained bottled horseradish

PROCEDURE:

In a large saucepan, place the heavy cream on a medium-low heat and allow the cream to come to a low boil. Stir the cream with a wooden spoon and keep an eye on the cream because it will expand as it comes to a boil. When reducing heavy cream it is always a good idea to use an oversized saucepan. As the cream settles to a low boil, add the bouillon cube and stir until dissolved. The cream should reduce by almost half its original volume and begin to thicken. When the sauce has reduced and thickened, remove from the heat, place in a room temperature mixing bowl, and whisk in the softened butter and cream cheese. Lastly, add the horseradish and serve immediately. Most heavy cream sauces cannot be refrigerated or reheated because the sauce will separate.

TOOLS

One two-quart saucepan, wooden spoon, wire whisk, measuring spoons and cup, cutting board and chef's knife.

Imperial Sauce

. . . .

YIELD: 1 QUART

INGREDIENTS:

1½ cups whole milk
8 tablespoons butter (1 stick)
6 tablespoons flour
1½ cups mayonnaise
½ teaspoon Worcestershire sauce
4 dashes of Tabasco sauce

½ cup finely diced green bell pepper, blanched
½ cup finely diced red bell pepper, blanched
1 tablespoon pickled capers
½ teaspoon white pepper
½ teaspoon Colman dry English mustard
2 whole extra large eggs

PROCEDURE:

In a saucepan, place the milk over a medium heat until just before a boil. In a separate saucepan melt the butter over a low heat. Add the flour to the melted butter to make a roux. Stir constantly until the flour is incorporated into the butter, making a smooth roux, then remove the roux from the heat and set aside. When the milk has reached a boil, add the smooth cooked roux and stir constantly over a medium heat until the sauce begins to thicken. At the first sign of a boil remove the thickened cream sauce from the heat and pour into a mixing bowl or a freestanding mixer.

To finish this sauce, place the thickened cream sauce into a freestanding mixer on a low speed. Let the mixer stir the thickened cream sauce, allowing the sauce to cool as well as maintain its smooth texture. Next, add the mayonnaise, Worcestershire sauce, Tabasco, blanched sweet bell peppers, capers and seasonings. Continue mixing the sauce and when somewhat cooled add the eggs and mix until the sauce is complete. Remove the sauce from the mixer and place in a shallow container and refrigerate until time of service.

TOOLS

. . . .

Two medium saucepans, two wire whisks, freestanding mixer, cutting board, chefs knife, measuring spoons and cups.

Coarse Ground Mustard Sauce

· ·

YIELD: 1 QUART

This sauce has so many uses it is hard to begin. A great sauce for meats, sausages, pork and game, it also suits many seafood dishes, especially grilled steak fish, like tuna or wahoo. This is one of our mother sauces at the restaurant even if it is not on the menus at the time.

INGREDIENTS:

2 cups whole milk
1 cup half-and-half cream
1 cube chicken bouillon
4 tablespoons butter
3 tablespoons flour

¼ cup course ground mustard (French Pommery)
½ cup dark Octoberfest beer
1 teaspoon salt
½ teaspoon white pepper

PROCEDURE:

In a saucepan place the milk, half-and-half, and bouillon cube over a medium heat until just under a boil. In a separate pan melt the butter over a low heat and add the flour to make a roux. Stir the roux constantly until smooth, then remove from heat. When the cream has come to a boil add the smooth cooked roux to the hot cream and stir constantly until the sauce begins to thicken. At the first sign of a boil remove from the heat and pour into a four-quart mixing bowl. In the mixing bowl add the mustard, beer, salt and pepper and stir until thoroughly combined. Taste the sauce to see if it needs more mustard, beer or salt.

Remember a recipe is only a blueprint; you can finish the rest.

TOOLS

· · · · · · · · · · · · ·

One two-quart saucepan, one-quart saucepan, four-quart mixing bowl, wire whisk, wooden spoon, measuring cup and spoons.

Pernod Cream Sauce

YIELD: ABOUT 2 CUPS

INGREDIENTS:

¾ cup whole milk

¾ cup half-and-half cream

2 tablespoons chicken stock

1 tablespoon hand-chopped fresh garlic

4 tablespoons butter

3 tablespoons flour

2 tablespoons Pernod, a licorice-flavored
  French apéritif

1 teaspoon white pepper

1 teaspoon salt

1 tablespoon butter, softened

2 tablespoons heavy cream

¼ cup fresh leeks, white part only, split
  lengthwise and cut in half moons

PROCEDURE:

In a saucepan over medium heat place the milk, half-and-half cream, chicken stock and chopped garlic and bring to a low boil. Next take the simmering cream and strain through a pasta strainer to remove the garlic pieces and other impurities then return the hot cream to the heat and back to a low simmering boil.

In a small saucepan melt the 4 tablespoons butter over a low heat and stir in the flour to make a roux. Cook the roux over a low heat until very smooth, then remove from heat and set aside. Now add the roux to the simmering cream and whip constantly until the sauce begins to thicken and returns to a boil. At the first sign of a boil remove the sauce from the heat and pour into a two-quart mixing bowl. Once again, all cream sauces should be removed from the saucepan as soon as it is taken off the heat.

Now let's flavor this sauce. Add the Pernod, white pepper and salt and taste. Remember, the Pernod flavor will grow in intensity, so let it rest before adding any more. Next, fold in the 1 tablespoon softened butter and heavy cream to give this sauce a satin finish, and lastly fold in the leeks. The onion flavor will enhance the sauce as well as give it a crunchy texture.

TOOLS

Measuring spoons and cup, cutting board, chef's knife, two-quart saucepan, smaller saucepan, whisk, wooden spoon, strainer and two-quart mixing bowl.

Pesto Cream Sauce

. . . .

YIELD: ABOUT 1½ CUPS

INGREDIENTS:

2 cups heavy cream
2 tablespoons A Pretty Traditional Pesto
  (see page 180)

2 tablespoons butter, softened
1 tablespoon cream cheese, softened
Pinch salt and white pepper

PROCEDURE:

In a saucepan place the heavy cream over a medium-high heat and bring to a boil, then lower the heat to a simmer and let the cream start to reduce. Use a wooden spoon occasionally to stir the reducing cream. The cream should not be left unattended while reducing because if it were to overflow there would be a fire hazard.

Be patient and let the cream reduce; this will take about 20 minutes or so. The goal is to have the water evaporate from the cream and as this occurs the cream will begin to self-thicken. As the cream begins to thicken, the appearance will change to a denser consistency and slower boil. It is now time to remove from the heat and place in a room temperature mixing bowl. Add the pesto, softened butter and cream cheese to the reduced cream and mix thoroughly. Adjust the seasoning to your taste but remember the pesto flavor will grow in intensity.

This sauce should be served immediately and is very hard to reuse because the cream will separate during refrigeration. If you want to try to save and reheat, use a double boiler to reheat until warm and serve.

TOOLS

. . . .

Measuring spoons and cup, cutting board, chef's knife, heavy saucepan, wooden spoon and rubber spatula.

Parmesan Cheese and Fresh Dill Cream Sauce

. . . .

YIELD: ABOUT 1 QUART

INGREDIENTS:

3 cups whole milk

2 cubes chicken bouillon

3 tablespoons butter

3 tablespoons flour

¼ pound Parmesan cheese, shaved

1 ounce sambuca or similar licorice-flavored liquor

½ teaspoon salt

¼ teaspoon white pepper

1 tablespoon finely chopped fresh dill

PROCEDURE:

In a four-quart saucepan place the milk and chicken bouillon over medium heat and bring just to a boil. In a separate saucepan melt the butter over a low heat and whisk in the flour to make a roux. Now, stir the roux constantly until smooth and then remove from the heat and set aside. When the heated milk has reached a boil, add the cooked roux to the hot milk and increase the heat to medium-high. Stir constantly until the sauce begins to thicken. At the first sign of a boil remove from heat and place the sauce in a large mixing bowl. The main reason for doing this is because any cream sauce has a tendency to scald the bottom of the pan. In order to prevent taking a chance on this affecting the sauce, it is best to remove from the original cooking container.

To make this a cheese sauce, add the Parmesan cheese and whisk until the cheese is melted and completely incorporated. Now, add the sambuca, salt, white pepper and fresh dill and stir again until all the ingredients are

thoroughly combined into the sauce. Taste the sauce, but please keep in mind the full dill flavor will not shine through until the sauce has cooled slightly. Adjust the seasonings or add more cheese to your liking.

This sauce will not appear to be very thick after removing from the stove but remember the cheese will also act as a thickening agent for this cream sauce.

TOOLS

. . . .

Measuring spoons and cup, cutting board, chef's knife, two saucepans, two wire whisks and a wooden spoon.

Basic Cream Sauce

. . . .

This basic cream sauce, a béchamel sauce is one of the mother sauces. Depending on who you talk to there are five or six mother sauces. I strongly believe the béchamel is the hardest for young culinarians to master. One of the chefs I learned from called the cream sauce "the lady of all sauces." The most delicate to make, the easiest to burn and a sauce that never forgets. Patience is the key to making any cream sauce. If the sauce is not allowed to reach the proper temperature before the thickening agent is introduced, only bad things will occur.

The addition of Parmesan cheese, fresh herbs and other items to a basic cream sauce can easily transform a basic sauce into many variations.

Raspberry Sauce

YIELD: ABOUT 1 PINT

INGREDIENTS:

2 cups frozen raspberries
¼ cup water
¼ cup sugar

1 tablespoon cornstarch
1 tablespoon lukewarm water

PROCEDURE:

In a small saucepan over a medium heat place the raspberries, ¼ cup water and sugar and bring to a low boil. In a small mixing bowl dilute the cornstarch with the 1 tablespoon lukewarm water. Add the diluted cornstarch to the low boiling raspberries and stir until the mixture begins to thicken. As the thickened raspberry sauce returns to a boil, remove from the heat and pour into a chilled mixing bowl. Place the bowl of thickened raspberry sauce on top of a larger bowl filled with ice. This is an ice bath and is meant to cool cooked products more rapidly. While cooling, take a hand mixer or emulsifier and blend the thickened raspberry sauce until smooth. When the sauce is cooled, refrigerate until time of service.

TOOLS

Measuring spoons and cup, small saucepan, three mixing bowls, whisk, rubber spatula, hand mixer or emulsifier and ladle.

Red Bean and Tasso Ham Sauce

YIELD: ABOUT 3 QUARTS

INGREDIENTS:

8 ounces Tasso ham, small cubed (see HINT)

2 quarts chicken stock or water (if using water, readjust seasoning as needed)

3 cups dried kidney or red beans

¾ cup finely diced yellow onion

2 medium-sized green bell peppers, finely diced

2 tablespoons blackening spice seasoning

2 cups V-8 juice

1 cup tomato juice

HINT

If Tasso is unavailable, use a similar smoked shoulder of pork seasoned with Cajun spice.

PROCEDURE:

Place the diced Tasso ham in a baking pan and cook in a preheated 350-degree oven for about 10 minutes. Remove from the oven and add the chicken stock and kidney beans and stir until thoroughly combined. Cover the pan with foil or lid and place back in the oven for about 40 minutes or until most of the liquid is absorbed and beans are cooked.

Remove from the oven and add the onion, bell pepper and blackened spice, stir the bean mixture, then recover for about 10 minutes. This time and heat should be enough to cook the onion and peppers until tenders. Once again remove the cover and add the V-8 and tomato juices to make the sauce. Taste and readjust the seasoning if needed. Remember the blackening spices flavor and heat will increase as the sauce settles. It is nice to make the blackening seasoning but there are excellent blackening spice mixes available for purchase, especially the Master Cajun Chef Paul.

TOOLS

Measuring spoons and cup, cutting board, chef's knife and baking pan.

Rémoulade Sauce

. . . .

YIELD: ABOUT 1 PINT

INGREDIENTS:

½ cup ketchup

¼ cup chili sauce

½ cup mayonnaise

1 tablespoon Grey Poupon mustard

¼ cup salad oil

1 tablespoon cracked black pepper

1 teaspoon cayenne pepper

½ teaspoon Colman's dry English mustard

¼ cup finely diced spring onions

1 tablespoon pickled capers

½ teaspoon Tabasco sauce

PROCEDURE:

In a large mixing bowl combine the ketchup, chili sauce, mayonnaise and Poupon mustard and whip until a smooth consistency. Next, slowly add the salad oil, whisking until thoroughly incorporated into the sauce. Now, fold in the spices, spring onions, capers and Tabasco sauce. Refrigerate until time of service and, depending on use, either serve chilled or at room temperature.

TOOLS

. . . .

Measuring spoons and cup, cutting board, chef's knife, mixing bowl, whisk and rubber spatula.

Traditional "River's Inn" Tartar Sauce

YIELD: ABOUT 1 PINT

INGREDIENTS:

1½ cups mayonnaise
1 tablespoon finely chopped fresh dill
Pinch of sugar

2 tablespoons lemon juice
½ cup sweet green pickle relish
1 tablespoon pickled capers

PROCEDURE:

In a mixing bowl place the mayonnaise, fresh dill, sugar and lemon juice, and whisk until smooth. Next, fold in the pickle relish and capers and whisk until thoroughly combined.

TOOLS

Measuring spoons and cup, cutting board, chef's knife, mixing bowl, whisk and rubber spatula.

Not So Traditional "Berret's" Tartar Sauce

YIELD: ABOUT 1 PINT

INGREDIENTS:

1½ cups mayonnaise
½ cup sweet red pepper relish

Juice of 2 lemons

PROCEDURE:

In a large mixing bowl place the mayonnaise, red pepper relish and lemon juice. Whisk until thoroughly combined. Keep refrigerated until time of service.

TOOLS

Measuring spoons and cup, cutting board, chef's knife, mixing bowl and whisk.

River's Inn and Berret's Steak Sauce

YIELD: ABOUT 1 PINT

INGREDIENTS:

1 cup cocktail sauce or seasoned ketchup
¼ cup molasses
2 tablespoons honey
2 tablespoons soy sauce

2 tablespoons Worcestershire sauce
2 tablespoons yellow mustard (like French's)
¼ tablespoon Montreal seasoning, a blend of garlic and pepper

PROCEDURE:

In a large mixing bowl place all the ingredients and whisk until thoroughly combined. This sauce is best served at room temperature with everything from beef, pork, chicken and a variety of seafood. It is best to refrigerate between uses.

TOOLS

Measuring spoons and cup, mixing bowl and whisk.

Creamy Sun-Dried Tomato Sauce

YIELD: 2 CUPS

INGREDIENTS:

4 ounces sun-dried tomatoes

1 cup water

2 cups heavy cream

½ tablespoon pureed or finely chopped fresh garlic

1 tablespoon pureed or finely chopped fresh shallots

½ teaspoon ground white pepper

1 tablespoon dry sherry

2 tablespoons butter, softened

4 ounces cream cheese, softened

PROCEDURE:

In a small mixing bowl place the sun-dried tomatoes and water, stir and let stand until the tomatoes are rehydrated. When the tomatoes are soft, remove from the water, strain and rinse to remove any excess salt.

In a two-quart saucepan over medium-high heat place the heavy cream, garlic puree, shallot puree and softened sun-dried tomatoes. Let the mixture come to a boil then reduce the heat to medium. As the cream comes to a low rolling boil, stir constantly with a wooden spoon. This should ensure the tomatoes will not stick to the bottom of the pan. Let the sun-dried cream mixture cook until it begins to self-thicken and reduces to half of its original volume. When the sauce has thickened remove from the heat, pour into a food processor and blend until smooth. Take the blended sun-dried tomato sauce and place in a mixing bowl and add the white pepper, sherry, butter and cream cheese. Whip the sauce until all the ingredients are thoroughly combined and smooth.

Taste the sauce to see if it needs more pepper, sherry or salt and then pour the sauce through a medium-fine strainer to remove any excess tomato skin from the sauce. Taste again and adjust the seasonings to your liking.

> ### TOOLS
>
> Measuring spoons and cup, cutting board, chef's knife, two saucepans, wooden spoon, food processor, two mixing bowls, medium-fine strainer and wire whisk.

Sweet Cream and Fresh Herb Sauce

. . . .

YIELD: 1½ CUPS

INGREDIENTS:

1 cup heavy cream
½ cube seafood or chicken bouillon
2 tablespoons butter, softened
   (unsalted preferably)

3 tablespoons cream cheese, softened
1 tablespoon fresh herbs, your choice of dill,
   thyme or basil, depending on the dish
Salt and white pepper

PROCEDURE:

In a saucepan over medium-low heat place the heavy cream and bring to a low boil. Be aware of the possibility of the cream expanding and boiling over the side of the pan. It is always a good idea to use an oversized pan when reducing heavy cream. The overflow of heavy cream is a very real fire hazard.

As the cream settles to a low boil add the bouillon and stir with a wooden spoon until dissolved. The use of a wooden spoon does not pull the heat out of the cream as a metal utensil would. The cream should reduce by half its original volume and begin to self-thicken. With the cream reduced and self-thickened, remove from the heat and place in a mixing bowl. Add the softened butter, cream cheese and fresh herbs and whisk until smooth. Season the cream sauce with salt and white pepper and serve immediately. Be aware the sauce cannot be refrigerated or reused.

> ## TOOLS
> . . . .
> *Two-quart saucepan, wooden spoon, wire whisk, measuring spoons and cup, cutting board, and chefs knife.*

DESSERTS

DESSERTS

· · · · · · · · · · ·

Crème Brûlée served with
Fresh Berries and Whipped Cream, 207

White Chocolate and Pecan Cheesecake
served with Caramel Sauce and Whipped Cream, 208

Grilled Pound Cake served with
Vanilla Ice Cream, Chocolate Sauce, Fresh Bananas,
Walnuts and Whipped Cream, 210

"Mudge Pie" served
with Chocolate Sauce,
Whipped Cream and Fresh Mint, 212

Key Lime Tart served with
Raspberry Sauce, Toasted Coconut,
Whipped Cream and Fresh Mint, 213

Crème Brûlée served with Fresh Berries and Whipped Cream

. . . .

YIELD: 12 SERVINGS

INGREDIENTS:

1 quart heavy cream
1 cup sugar, divided
½ teaspoon pure vanilla extract
½ vanilla bean, split in half lengthwise
1 whole egg

2 pints fresh berries, strawberries or blueberries
3 cups fresh whipped cream
12 sprigs fresh mint

PROCEDURE:

In a saucepan over a medium heat place the heavy cream, ¾ cup of sugar, the extract and the split vanilla bean. The goal is to just dissolve the sugar into the cream and extract as much of the inside of the vanilla bean as possible. Please do not let come to a boil. After the sugar is dissolved, remove from heat and set side for a couple of minutes. In a large mixing bowl, place the eggs and whip until completely smooth. Remove the bean from the hot cream and scrape the inside of the vanilla bean into the eggs. Slowly add the warm cream to the eggs. This is called tempering, bringing the hot and cold mixtures together slowly and arriving at a medium temperature. When all the cream has been incorporated into the egg mixture, whip until thoroughly combined.

Pour the crème brûlée mixture into individual baking dishes, about five to six ounces each. Place the dishes in a roasting pan and fill the roasting pan halfway with water, surrounding the baking dishes. This is called a hot water bath and will slow the cooking temperature and time. Place in a preheated 300-degree oven for about 45 minutes. Remove from the roasting pan and let sit at room temperature for a few minutes before refrigerating. Then refrigerate until ready to serve.

When ready to serve, sprinkle the remaining ¼ cup of sugar on top of the chilled crème brûlée. With a gas propane torch, carefully "brûlée" or burn the sugar until brown and crispy. Finally, garnish with the fresh berries, whipped cream and mint.

TOOLS

. . . .

Measuring cups and spoons, cutting board, chef's knife, saucepan, mixing bowl, two wire whips, ladle, roasting pan and propane torch.

White Chocolate and Pecan Cheesecake
served with Caramel Sauce and Whipped Cream

. . . .

YIELD: 8 TO 10 SERVINGS

INGREDIENTS: *(for Cheesecake Filling)*

1½ pounds ricotta cheese

1 pound cream cheese

1¼ cups sugar

4 whole eggs

¼ cup flour

¾ cup pecan pieces, toasted and coarsely ground

INGREDIENTS: *(for Crust)*

2 cups crushed Oreo cookies

Nonstick cooking spray

INGREDIENTS: *(for Ganache Topping)*

¼ pound white chocolate, room temperature

½ cup heavy cream

ACCOMPANIMENTS: *(to Service)*

1 cup Caramel Sauce (see page 186)

1½ cups fresh whipped cream

PROCEDURE:

In a freestanding mixer, place the two cheeses and sugar. Blend at medium speed until smooth, then slowly add the eggs and then the flour. Continue mixing on a low speed until smooth. Slowly add the ground pecans to complete the cheesecake filling.

Place the crushed Oreo cookies in the bottom of the springform pan and spray the top of the cookies with the cooking spray, then gently press down on the cookies. Coat the sides of the pan with the cooking spray and slowly pour the cheesecake filling into the pan. With a rubber spatula, gently pat the top of the cheesecake to settle down the filling and make very smooth. Place the cheesecake in a preheated 300-degree oven and bake for 75 to 90 minutes, rotating halfway through the cooking cycle. After removing the cheesecake from the oven,

> ### TOOLS
> . . . .
>
> *Hand mixer or stand-up table mixer, two two-quart mixing bowls, wire whip, rubber spatula, measuring cups and spoons, a ten-inch springform pan, ladle, chef's knife, cutting board and pot.*

White Chocolate and Pecan Cheesecake continued

let it rest for approximately 30 minutes at room temperature before refrigerating. This will avoid any cracking of the top of the cake due to extreme temperature changes.

Fill a large pot half full with water and bring to a boil. In a large mixing bowl, place the white chocolate and heavy cream. Then place the mixing bowl on top of the pot filled with boiling water. This is called a double boiler. The chocolate and cream will melt slowly over the boiling water and should never burn. When the chocolate is completely melted and the cream is completely incorporated, remove from the heat and set aside. This is the ganache.

Remove the cheesecake from the refrigerator and pour the white chocolate ganache over the entire cake. Return to the refrigerator for at least 3 hours before serving.

To "Plate-Up", place a slice of the white chocolate cheesecake on the plate. Drizzle with the Caramel Sauce and top with the fresh whipped cream.

Grilled Pound Cake served with Vanilla Ice Cream, Chocolate Sauce, Fresh Bananas, Walnuts and Whipped Cream

. . . .

YIELD: ABOUT 12 SERVINGS

INGREDIENTS: *(for Pound Cake)*

2 cups cake flour, sifted

1 teaspoon baking powder

¾ pound butter (3 sticks), softened

½ cup solid vegetable shortening (Crisco)

1¼ cups half-and-half cream

3 cups confectioners' sugar

4 whole eggs

½ tablespoon vanilla extract

Nonstick cooking spray

ACCOMPANIMENTS: *(for Service)*

1½ cups vanilla ice cream

1½ cups Chocolate Sauce (see page 187)

2 large bananas, sliced

1 cup chopped walnut pieces

1½ cups fresh whipped cream

1 bunch fresh mint sprigs

PROCEDURE:

Place the flour, baking powder, butter and vegetable shortening in a freestanding mixer and whip on medium speed until creamy. Add the half-and-half cream and confectioners' sugar. Reduce the speed to low. Add the whole eggs and vanilla extract and whip until a smooth batter has formed. The use of a rubber spatula will enable you to scrape down the sides and bottom of the bowl and avoid any pockets of butter or shortening.

Spray the bottom and sides of a loaf bread pan with cooking spray, sprinkle with flour and evenly pour the batter into the pan. Another way to ensure the cake does not stick to the pan is to lay a wax paper liner throughout the pan. Place the pound cake into a preheated 350-degree oven and bake for 1 hour, 15 minutes, rotating the cake halfway through the cooking period. After removing the pound cake from the oven, let rest in the pan for about 15 minutes. Remove from the pan by simply turning the pan over and hopefully letting the cake slip right out. If it does not slip right out you may

> ## TOOLS
> . . . .
> *Measuring spoons and cup, cutting board and chef's knife, freestanding mixer or hand held and a mixing bowl, bread pan, ladle, rubber spatula and ice cream scoop.*

Grilled Pound Cake continued

have to tap on the bottom of the pan to get the cake to release. Refrigerate the cake until time of service.

To "Plate-Up", when ready to serve, cut about 1½-inch slices of the cake and lay the slices down on a hot grill. If a grill is not available, heat in the oven for a few minutes until hot. Next, place the hot pound cake on the plate and top with a generous scoop of vanilla ice cream. Pour the Chocolate Sauce over top of the ice cream and garnish with banana slices, chopped walnuts, whipped cream and fresh mint.

"Mudge Pie" served with Chocolate Sauce, Whipped Cream and Fresh Mint

YIELD: ABOUT 12 SERVINGS

A short story about this dessert: it is a traditional ice cream dessert known as a Mud Pie. In the middle 1980's, primarily based on a friend's observation of my attitude at the time, he thought that it should be called "Curmudgeon Pie."

INGREDIENTS:

1 cup graham cracker crumbs
1 cup ground Oreo cookie crumbs
1 cup sliced almonds
2 tablespoons butter, softened
Nonstick cooking spray

½ gallon vanilla ice cream, softened
½ gallon chocolate ice cream, softened
½ gallon butter pecan ice cream, softened
1½ cups Chocolate Sauce (see page 187)
1½ cups fresh whipped cream
12 sprigs fresh mint

PROCEDURE:

In a large mixing bowl, combine the graham cracker crumbs, crushed Oreo cookies, sliced almonds and softened butter. Mix until thoroughly combined then set aside at room temperature. Spray the bottom and sides of a false bottom or spring form pan with the cooking spray. Line the inside of the pan with wax paper, bottom and over the sides. Sprinkle half of the graham cracker mixture on the bottom of the pan and gently press down to form a base. Place the pan in the freezer to solidify.

In a freestanding mixer, place the softened vanilla ice cream and blend until smooth. Using a rubber spatula, spoon the smooth ice cream on top of the graham cracker base in a long layer. Return the pan to the freezer until solid; repeat this with the other two layers of ice cream, placing the chocolate layer in the center. After the last butter pecan layer is placed, sprinkle the other half of the graham cracker mixture on top. Fold over the wax paper and gently press down. Return to the freezer until time of service.

TOOLS

Measuring spoons and cup, cutting board, chef's knife, mixing bowl, rubber spatula, false bottom or spring form pan, freestanding mixer and ladle.

When ready to serve, remove the pan from the freezer, turn upside down and gently remove the ice cream cake from the pan. Place a pool of warm chocolate sauce on the bottom of a plate. Cut a wedge from the ice cream cake and set the slice on top of the chocolate sauce. Top with whipped cream and a sprig of fresh mint.

Key Lime Tart served with Raspberry Sauce, Toasted Coconut, Whipped Cream and Fresh Mint

· ·

YIELD: 8 TO 10 SERVINGS

INGREDIENTS:

5 egg yolks
1½ cups condensed milk (Eagle brand)
½ cup "real" Key Lime juice
Nonstick cooking spray
½ cup ground graham cracker crumbs
¼ cup flour

½ cup crushed Oreo cookies
1 pint Raspberry Sauce (see page 198)
2 cups fresh whipped cream
¼ cup toasted coconut
8-10 sprigs fresh mint

PROCEDURE:

In a mixing bowl, place the egg yolks, condensed milk and lime juice. Whip until thoroughly combined. Spray the bottom and sides of a ten-inch false bottom tart pan or springform pan with the cooking spray. In another mixing bowl, combine the graham cracker crumbs, flour and crushed Oreo cookies and hand toss until the crust is complete. Pour the crust into the bottom of the tart pan and gently press to the bottom of the pan.

Next, slowly pour or ladle the key lime batter into the baking pan. When the batter is settled in the pan evenly, gently take a spoon or rubber spatula and settle or smooth out any ripples on the top of the tart. Place the tart in a preheated 300-degree oven for approximately 20 minutes. The length of time depends on depth of pan. The finished tart should have a slightly firm texture and appearance. After removing the tart from the oven, let rest at room temperature for about 10 minutes before refrigerating.

It is time to "Plate-Up." Ladle a pool of raspberry sauce on the bottom of the plate and place a slice of the key lime tart on the sauce. Top the tart with whipped cream, a sprinkle of toasted coconut and a sprig of fresh mint.

TOOLS

· · · · · · · · · · · · · ·

Two two-quart mixing bowls, wire whisk, wooden spoon, 10-inch tart pan, rubber spatula and measuring spoons and cup.

INDEX

. . . .